A 2023-2024 Starting-Point Guide

Lyon, France

Plus the Saône and Rhône Confluence Region

Barry Sanders – writing as:

B G Preston

Lyon, France

ISBN: 9798863794860

3rd edition – October 2023 - AR

Acknowledgements: The author greatly appreciates Sandra Sanders' contributions and guidance.

Photography: Maps and photos in the Starting-Point Guides are a mix of those taken by the author, Adobe Media, Shutterstock, Wikimedia, and Google maps. No photograph or map in this work should be used without checking with the author first.

Cover photography by Rogue Teacher Photos

www.RogueTeacherPhotos.com.

Forward and Some Notes from the Author on the Starting-Point Guides Approach and Coverage.

What we look for in a travel guidebook can vary by each individual. Some travelers want great details into the history of every monument or museum, others may want details on area restaurants. This guide's coverage is a bit broader in approach. The goal of every Starting-Point Guide is to help orient you to the city and area and to gain an understanding of its layout, how to get around and highlights of the town's treasures and what is nearby.

Overviews are provided on the town, suggested lodging, points-of-interest, travel, and the area. Few details are provided on restaurants and shops or historical details on monuments.

The end goal is for you to come away from your visit having a good understanding of what is here, what the town is like and not feel that you have missed out on leading sights and attractions.

Happy Travels, *B G Preston*

Chapters & Contents

Preface & Some Suggestions 6

1: Lyon – France's Second City 10

2: One Day in Lyon Suggested Itinerary...........................23

3: Traveling to Lyon 26

4: Lyon's Points of Interest 32

5: Traboules, Bouchons, Silk & Murals.........................66

6: Getting Around in Lyon 78

7: City Passes and Tours...88

8: Where to Stay in Lyon..93

9: Nearby Day Trips from Lyon 104

10: Day Trips Further Afield.......................................115

Appendix: Helpful Online References 123

Index 128

Starting-Point Travel Guides 129

LYON

View of Lyon's Basilica of Notre-Dame de Fourvière from Place Bellecour.

Preface & Some Suggestions

This Starting-Point guide is intended for travelers who wish to really get to know a city and area and not just make it one quick stop on a tour through France or Europe. Oriented around the concept of using Lyon as a basecamp for several days, this handbook provides guidance on sights both in Lyon and in the nearby wine country and neighboring towns.

Itinerary Suggestions: If your travel schedule allows plan on staying at least 2 nights in Lyon. Ideally, you will be able to stay as many as four or five nights.

This is an area with a wonderful variety of sights outside town. Several days are needed to gain even a moderate understanding of what this area has to offer.

Strive to leave one day open and unplanned near the end of your stay. Build in a day in which you have not pre-booked any excursions or planned major activities.

The reason for this is that, once there, you will discover places which you either want to revisit or learn about new places which appeal to you. If you have a full schedule, you will lose this luxury.

Just have one day? Check chapter 2 for a suggested itinerary for a one day visit to Lyon.

Consider a City Card: When staying in a city filled with attractions, purchasing a City Card can be advantageous.

Acquire one if you are likely to visit multiple attractions. Do not acquire one if you only want to visit one or two attractions during your stay.

These passes can always be purchased in the Tourist Office and are available online prior to your trip. When visiting Lyon, you will have the option of purchasing the City Card in increments of 1, 2, 3 or 4 days. See chapter 7 for details.

Visit the Tourist Office: Lyon's main Tourist Information Office is conveniently located. It is situated at Place Bellecour, a huge and historic plaza central to many of the attractions you are likely to want to visit.

> Lyon Tourist Office Website:
> En.Lyon-France.com

Obtain information on available tours and places to visit. Even if you have done substantial research prior to your trip, it is likely you will learn of opportunities which you had not previously uncovered.

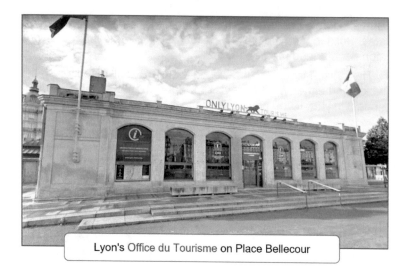

Lyon's Office du Tourisme on Place Bellecour

Download Some Apps: With the incredible array of apps for Apple and Android devices, almost every detail you will need to have a great trip is available up to and including where to find public toilets. The following are a few apps used and recommended by the author.

- Lyon Smart Guide: Audio guide and interactive maps to Lyon's attractions.

- Lyon Map and Walks: Developed by "GPS my City." This firm does a great job of providing local walking tours and suggested walking routes in Lyon and the other cities they provide this app for.[1]

- Lyon Metro & Tram Map: Lyon has a comprehensive transportation network, and this app goes a long way in helping you understand how to use the system and which routes to travel to reach your destinations.

---

[1] Maps in this guide vs Apps: The apps cited here, such as the Lyon Map and Walks app, provide far more details than printed maps, such as those within this guide can do.

- Lyon Metro Guide and Tramway Map. Like the above Metro and Tram Map app, this provides details on the area's transportation routes.

- SNCF Trains: This is the primary regional train service in France. Use this app to see schedules, routes, and purchase rail tickets for travel into Lyon and other cities.

- Rome2Rio: An excellent way to research all travel options including rental cars, trains, flying, ferry, and taxi. The app provides the ability to purchase tickets directly online.

- Trip Advisor: Probably the best overall app for finding details on most hotels, restaurants, excursions, and attractions.

- Flush: A very helpful app which provides guidance on where to find public toilets.

The Lyon Metro and Tram App helps you navigate the city's transportion network.

1: Lyon – France's Second City

Lyon [2] is frequently referred to as France's Second City. The city's promoters state that Lyon is the second most popular destination in France after Paris. Lyon is one of the oldest cities in France with history dating back to its founding by the Romans in 43 BC. The historic Le Vieux Lyon section of town is a UNESCO World Heritage site.

In size, Lyon, is France's 2nd largest metropolitan area and the 3rd largest city. Only Paris and Marseille have larger populations living within their city limits. It is a vital center of commerce and culture in addition to having the reputation of being the capital of French cuisine.

View of central Lyon - looking over the Saône River.

---

[2] Lyon pronunciation. The normal English pronunciation for Lyon is simply "LEE own" with emphasis on the "Lee." This is often confused with Leon, Spain in which Leon's pronunciation is "Lay own."

Lyon, like many cities, is largely defined by its rivers and topography. Sitting at the confluence of the Saône and Rhône, this area was a natural hub for trading and transportation coming up from the Mediterranean in the south. This trading history goes back thousands of years. When visiting here, you will have

Lyon has more Renaissance-era buildings than any other city in Europe.

opportunities to take scenic boat tours and walk along the banks of one or both rivers. The scenery from the bridges which cross over the Saône is beautiful, so have your camera at hand.

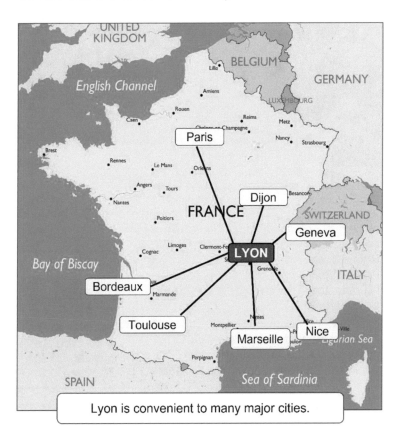

Lyon is convenient to many major cities.

Lyon is the capital of the French district known as Auvergne-Rhône-Alpes. This region stretches east to Switzerland, south to Provence, and west to the Nouvelle-Aquitaine region which includes Bordeaux and Biarritz.

Place Bellecour
Located in the heart of the Presqu'île district.

When visiting Lyon for the first time, you soon realize that much of the historic area rests on a flat strip called the Presqu'île[3] which lies between the historic Saône and Rhône rivers. Across the Saône from the Presqu'île, the city rises dramatically uphill with the beautiful basilica towering over the town.

The flat Presqu'île contains much of the historic area and is considered by many to be the heart of the city. This peninsula between two rivers holds

The large "Place Bellecour" is officially "Kilometer 0" of Lyon. All distances to and from Lyon are calculated from here.

---

[3] Presqu'île: This term literally means peninsula or a combination of the two French terms for "almost" and "island."

many of the sights which visitors will want to see. A great place to start is Place Bellecour, one of the largest open squares in Europe. This is where the Tourist Office is located.

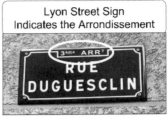

Lyon Street Sign
Indicates the Arrondissement

Lyon's arrondissements are divided into 9 political subdivisions. When touring the city, almost everything you visit will be in the 1st, 2nd and 5th arrondissements as depicted in the map below.

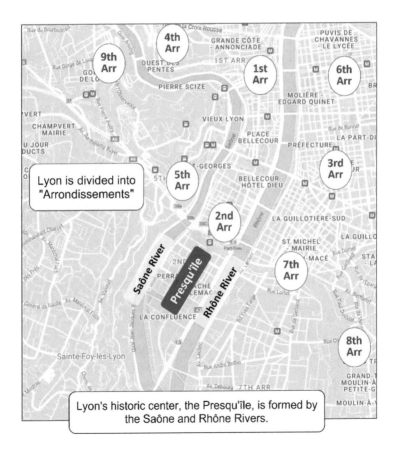

Lyon is divided into "Arrondissements"

Lyon's historic center, the Presqu'île, is formed by the Saône and Rhône Rivers.

The previous map depicts the general layout of these arrondissements. When asking for directions from locals, it is common for you to be instructed to go to a certain arrondissement, so having a basic understanding of this structure can be helpful.

Lyon's Historical Center
The Presqu'île - bordered by the Saône and Rhône Rivers
Photo Source: Google Earth

The 2nd Arrondissement: Often just referred to as the Presqu'île. This is where you may want to consider starting your explorations of the city and area. The 2nd stretches south to the "confluence", the point where the two rivers come together.

The 1st Arrondissement. This is just north of the 2nd arr. It is the smallest but holds the important Place des Terreaux, the Hôtel de Ville and the Museum of Fine Arts (Musée des Beaux-Arts).

Place des Jacobins
Located between the Saône and Rhône rivers.

The 5th Arrondissement is where some of the most impressive historical structures can be found. Situated on a steep hill which overlooks the Saône and the Presqu'île, are ancient Roman ruins, the charming Vieux Lyon area, and the notable basilica, and the cathedral. See chapter 4 which outlines the highlights of this area.

This is a city of culture with hundreds of events occurring each year. The museums here offer an incredible range from

 Accessibility Caution

Some areas of Lyon, especially in the historic Vieux Lyon (5th arr) have narrow cobblestone streets which can be problematic for individuals in wheelchairs and scooters.

Interpol, the international police organization, is based in the 6th arrondissement

the expected and traditional to the very modern such as the Museum of the Confluence. Cinema and its development have deep roots in Lyon and museums here honor that history.

Parks and squares, large and small, are everywhere. Many small squares such as the Place des Jacobins offer the visitor a delightful array of shops and restaurants. Other parks, such as the beautiful Parc de la Tête d'Or offer visitors hundreds of acres of gardens to explore.

Primary Areas to Explore: Lyon's historical treasures are largely found in the two sections of the Presqu'île and the neighboring Vieux Lyon which is situated immediately across the Saône. The two areas are connected by several bridges over the river. The bridges provide wonderful photo opportunities of the Saône river below and the hilly Vieux Lyon to the west.

Looking west toward Vieux Lyon. across the Saône River.

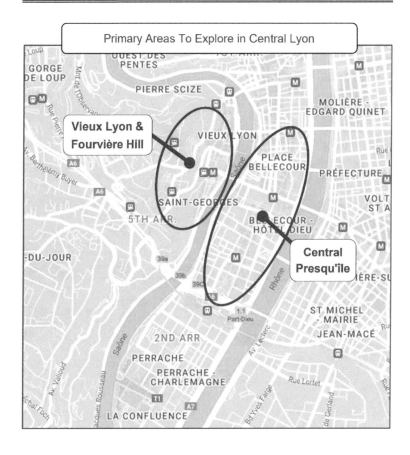

Primary Areas To Explore in Central Lyon

The Presqu'île: The Presqu'île is a long, flat area stretching from the confluence of the two rivers north to the central heart of town in the 1st arrondissement. This is where the Place des Terreaux and Hôtel de Ville are located.

Much of this peninsula was once a swampy area between the two rivers. In the 18th century, a substantial project was initiated to drain the marshes and connect what was once an island to other areas.

This peninsula is now the heart of the city and where most major events happen. Here you can enjoy beautiful 19th century architecture, broad boulevards, museums, numerous shops, restaurants, and bars.

The Place des Terreaux on Lyon's Presqu'île

When starting your visit to Lyon, consider heading directly to Place Bellecour, a large red-dirt square which includes the tourist office. Most points of interest on the Presqu'île will be found near the Place Bellecour and in the stretch just north of this large square. The one notable exception to this is the ultra-modern Musèe des Confluences which is at the southern tip of the peninsula. Details on this museum may be found in chapter 4.

Vieux Lyon: In the 15th through 17th centuries, Lyon had a prestigious and thriving silk industry. Much of this industry was centered in the area known as Vieux Lyon. This section is the largest Renaissance district of Lyon and is one of the largest in all of Europe.

When the silk industry was at its peak, the area held the homes of many rich merchant families from across France, Germany, and Italy. These families built luxurious homes in the renaissance styles and nearly 300 of these homes remain today.

> Vieux Lyon was the first location in France to be protected as a national cultural site.

Among the numerous historical delights found here are silk shops, the intriguing network of hidden passages called traboules, and Lyon's unique dining experience, the bouchons. These are described further in chapter 5.

Vieux Lyon is an area with many intriguing small streets to explore.

In addition to the traboules, silk shops, and bouchons, take time to explore such treasures as the funiculars, an ancient Roman amphitheater, a magnificent basilica, and a beautiful cathedral.

~ ~ ~ ~ ~ ~

Some Interesting Facts About Lyon:

- **A leader of French Cuisine**: Lyon is often called the capital of France gastronomy. While other city leaders may want to argue this point, there is a lot to be said about the range and quality of dining here. There are over 4,000 restaurants here including 9 with Michelin stars. If you are, like the author, reluctant to shell out a large volume of Euros for a meal, head to one of the many Bouchons in Vieux Lyon. These are typically small, family-run establishments which focus on local cuisine.

- **The Capital of Ancient France**: For centuries, during the Roman period, ancient France was known as Gaul. This region was divided into three parts and Lyon was the capital of all three areas. Today, the several ruins of Roman theaters attest to this.

- **The Little Prince**: The author, Antoine de Saint-Exupéry, of the world-wide best seller "*The Little Prince*" was from here. In addition to being an author, he was a pilot who died during WWII. Today Lyon's airport is named after him and there is a monument to him in the large central plaza Place Bellecour. Copies of this book in several languages are readily available in bookshops in Lyon.

- **Cinema was Created Here**: The Lumière Brothers of Lyon created what was then called the Cinematograph. Their first movie was filmed in Lyon. Today, there is a museum in their original studio. This museum is a short distance west from central Lyon. www.Instit-Lumiere.org. (Check before going as it has been closed for renovation.)

- **Largest City-Center Mall in Europe?** If you come to Lyon by train, chances are you will arrive at the Part-Dieu station. This same facility also is home to a mall which many sources claim is the biggest mall (within a city center) in all of Europe. Even if some sources differ with this assessment, this mall is huge.

And, yes, Europe does have many larger malls, just not in the heart of the city as the Part-Dieu shopping center is.

- Sports and Stadiums: Even if you are not into sports, there is something to be said about the fun of watching the local citizens go nuts during a football/soccer game. Roughly midway between downtown Lyon and the airport is the huge Groupama Stadium (59,000 seating capacity which is also known as Parc Olympique Lyon-

Groupama Stadium
Photo source: Wikimedia Commons

nais) where you can watch some of the world's top men and women's soccer teams play. The stadium is easily reached by tram from central Lyon. Check out www.Olvallee.fr for the current game schedule.

- World's First Funicular: This popular mode of transportation can be found in many hilly cities, but the first one was created for Lyon in 1882 and is still in operation. It can be found in the historic Vieux Lyon section of town and takes riders directly up to the cathedral.

Climate and When to Visit Lyon: Like most areas in Europe, your best times to visit Lyon are Spring, early Summer and Fall, especially if you wish to avoid crowds. In the Fall, the city is much less crowded with cooler autumn weather.

Lyon sits roughly at 600 feet elevation (180 meters). This slight elevation combined with its position between the Mediterranean to the south and the Alps to the east, creates an overall climate that is warm and temperate. Rain chance is steady throughout the year.

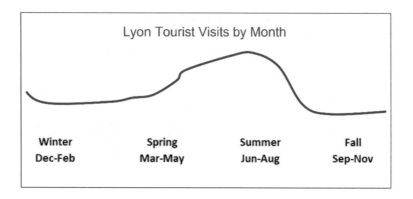

Average Area Climate by Month			
Month	Avg High	Avg Low	Avg Precip
Jan	45 F / 7 C	34 F /1 C	1.9 inches
Feb	48 F / 9 C	35 F /2 C	1.6 inches
Mar	57 F /14 C	40 F /4 C	1.9 inches
Apr	63 F /17 C	45 F /7 C	2.7 inches
May	71 F /21 C	52 F /11 C	3.2 inches
Jun	78 F /26 C	59 F /15 C	2.9 inches
Jul	83 F /28 C	63 F /17 C	2.7 inches
Aug	82 F /28 C	62 F /17 C	2.6 inches
Sep	74 F / 23 C	55 F /13 C	3.2 inches
Oct	64 F /18 C	49 F /10 C	3.9 inches
Nov	53 F /11 C	41 F / 5 C	3.4 inches
Dec	46 F / 8 C	36 F /2 C	2.1 inches

If you will be here for just one day and do not have a specific objective in mind such as a particular museum or restaurant, consider an agenda similar to the following. If you follow these guidelines, you will come away with a good overview and feel of Lyon and its treasures.

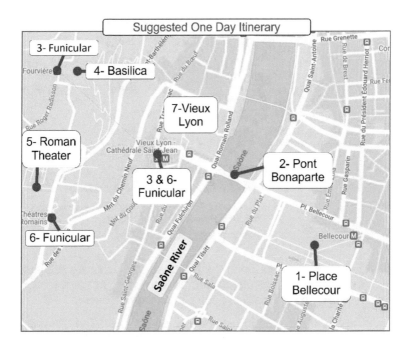

1. Start at Place Bellecour: This large plaza is the focal point of the area between the Saône and Rhône Rivers, known as the Presqu'ile. The Tourist Office is here, and the square is one of the largest in France. For travel convenience, the Metro stops here and there is underground parking if you are driving.

2. Walk to Vieux Lyon: Take a 6-to-10-minute walk west over the Saône River ending up in Lyon's old town, known as Vieux Lyon. The route takes you over the attractive Pont Bonaparte (Bridge) with great views of the city from the river.

This route crosses the Saône via the Pont Bonaparte
Photo source: Basilio-Wikimedia Commons

3. Ride the Funicular up to the Basilica: Once you are in Vieux Lyon, ride the funicular up the hill and come out at a station adjacent to the Basilica, Lyon's most iconic treasure.

4. Explore the Basilique Notre Dame de Fourvièr: The hill which looms over Vieux Lyon is known as Fourvière. The Basilica is a magnificent building to explore. Allow at least one hour to view this beautiful structure. Afterward, take time to enjoy the

views of Lyon below you and browse the many shops. There are some restaurants here and a nice park to relax with a meal.[4]

5. Walk to the Roman Ruins: Take a short 3-to-5-minute walk to the Roman ruins, the Théâtre Gallo Romain de Lyon Fourvière. There is also an excellent museum, the Lugdunum, here.

6. Take a Funicular back down to Vieux Lyon: There is another funicular line near the bottom of the Roman Ruins. This line takes riders back to the same point in Vieux Lyon where the other line departed from.

7. Explore Vieux Lyon: This is Lyon's Old Town and a great place to spend time exploring some of the noted Traboules (hidden passageways). Catch lunch or dinner in one of the many bouchons. (Small restaurants). While here, consider going into one of the museums such as the Puppetry or Cinema Miniatures Museum.

8. End your day: When you are done exploring, head off to your hotel or transportation site.

---

[4] Lyon Points of Interest. Information on Lyon's Basilica and other points of interest may be found in Chapter 4 of this guide.

3: Traveling to Lyon

Located north of Marseille and south of Paris, Lyon's central location is easy to reach. The travel guidance provided here assumes you will be coming to Lyon by train or airplane.

Should you choose to drive, this city and area are easy to navigate. The streets in and around central Lyon are well laid out and there are multi-lane highways leading into and out of the metropolitan area.

Trains and flights into the city are frequent, easy, and generally convenient to your needs. If you are booking travel to and from Lyon on your own, use trains if possible. The scenery along the way is beautiful and you can travel in a relaxed mode. Taking the train can often be faster than flying even though the actual transportation time can be longer. Trains take you directly from the center of one city to the center of another, plus you have minimal check-in time to deal with.

Arriving by Train: Lyon has several train stations. Two of them account for most traffic and are the stations you will likely use. Gare[5] Part-Dieu and Gare Lyon Perrache.

---

[5] Gare: This is the French term for a train station.

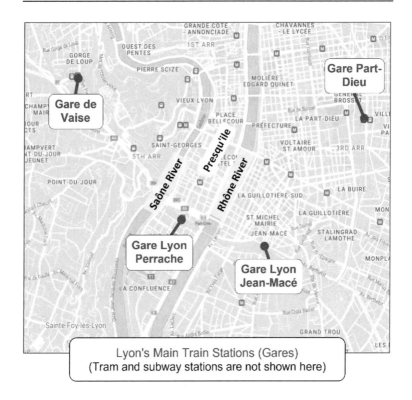

Lyon's Main Train Stations (Gares)
(Tram and subway stations are not shown here)

<u>Gare Part-Dieu:</u> The biggest and busiest station in Lyon and where the TGV trains[6] come in and depart from. There is also a large shopping mall connected to this station. Most trips from major cities such as Paris or Marseille will arrive at this station.

This station is in the 3rd arrondissement, which is just east of the Rhône River and, for most of us, is not a convenient walk into town. It is approximately a 10-minute taxi ride from this station to the center of Presqu'île.

Lyon's tram system services this train station. Depending on where you are staying in Lyon, it may be beneficial to utilize this modern system. See chapter 6 for details on Lyon's tram system.

---

[6] TGV trains: This is the high-speed train system in France.

27

The Gare Lyon Perrache: Situated on Lyon's Presqu'île. Many regional and local trains utilize this station. When taking day trips to nearby towns and villages, the trains you will take may depart from here.

Some of the high-speed TGV trains make a stop at this station before stopping at Part-Dieu. The tram system also stops here, making it convenient for many to travel from this train station to the vicinity of their lodging.

Walking time from this station to Place Bellecour and the numerous hotels near there is under twenty minutes.

Arriving from Paris by Train: A common route for travelers is to travel from Paris to Lyon. Two options for train travel are available for this.

- From Central Paris: Most of the trains from Paris are high-speed TGV and most are non-stop. The trip is typically under three hours.

  There are several train stations in Paris. Trains to Lyon depart out of the appropriately named 'Gare Lyon' station. This station is in the 12th Arrondissement, a short distance southeast from the center of Paris.

  Most TGV trains traveling to Lyon head directly to Lyon's Part-Dieu station. Some will give you the opportunity to stop in Lyon's Perrache station.

  There are several large train stations in Paris. When departing Paris, it is important to know that you are utilizing the Paris Gare Lyon station. You cannot simply tell a taxi driver to "Take me to the train station."

- From Charles de Gaulle Airport (CDG): This is a convenient way to travel as the train station is centrally located in this Paris airport. There is no need to first travel into central Paris to catch a train from there.

  The highspeed train does provide service directly from the Paris airport to Lyon. It is not necessary to change trains en route.

Booking Train Tickets. Given the popularity of travel to Lyon from Paris, advance purchase should be considered, especially in high season. If you have not purchased train tickets in advance, convenient ticket booths are available at the train station.

Several online services are available to book in advance including:

- SNCF.com – France's national rail service. Using them provides the advantage of being able to make changes in the station if problems arise.

- Ticket Resellers – several online agencies allow you to book tickets through them and may provide the convenience of booking other forms of transportation or lodging at the same time. Leading resources for this include:

  o www.rome2Rio.com (Author favorite)

  o www.TrainLine.com

  o www.RailEurope.com

Arriving by Air: The Lyon airport, "Lyon Saint-Exupéry" (LYS), is located on the eastern outskirts of the city. It is named after the author of the famed work, *The Little Prince.*

You should plan on a trip of roughly 30 minutes from the airport into town, regardless of the mode of transportation.

Lyon's airport was awarded "Europe's Best Airport" for 2019.

Taxi or Limo: Unless you are on a tight budget, consider taking a taxi (or UBER) from the airport. The huge advantage of doing this is the driver will take you and your luggage directly to your lodging. Another advantage is you will not have to wrestle with your luggage as you work your way on and off trams or buses.

Lyon's "Rhône Express" tram connects the airport to the city at the Part Dieu train station.

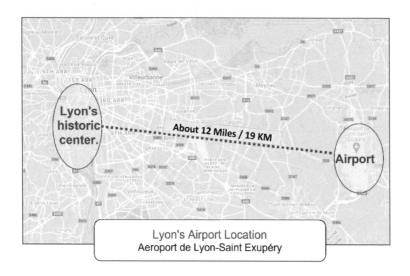

Lyon's Airport Location
Aeroport de Lyon-Saint Exupéry

The cost for a taxi from the airport into central Lyon should range between 60 to 75€ (Euro) plus tip. Pre-booking your ride is not necessary. If you prefer, several online services are available for you to book a ride in advance. One popular option is a service called "Welcome Pickups" (WelcomePickups.com). If you utilize this service, a car will be waiting for you with an English-speaking driver. The cost is similar to taking a taxi.

Trams from the Airport: Lyon has an excellent tram service which services the airport in addition to much of the city.If you wish to take the tram, it departs directly from the lower level of Lyon's airport arrivals area.

This shuttle-tram only takes you as far as Lyon's Part-Dieu train station. From this point, you will need to catch a taxi, another tram, or walk to your destination. This tram departs every 15 or 30 minutes, depending on the time of the day.

Cost of the airport tram is roughly 16€ per person each way with a discount for purchasing a roundtrip (return) ticket. The tickets may be purchased from kiosks at the airport or at the Part-Dieu train station.

If you are traveling with two or more people, taxis continue to be a better alternative. Travel time is roughly the same and a taxi can take you directly to your lodging while the shuttle does not.

Rhone Express Website: www.RhonExpress.fr

The sights in Lyon range from the traditional and expected museums to unique treasures. There are even some specialty museums such as one focused on puppetry and another displaying miniatures in cinema which add some fun to a visit of this city.

The following map and table provide a summary list of suggested sights in town. These sights are organized by the area of town they are in. Some specialty destinations such as Lyon's traboules are in later chapters.

Vieux Lyon and Fourvière Hill: The primary "Old Town" of Lyon where the basilica, cathedral and numerous museums may be found.

Presqu'ile-Central: The heart of Lyon which has the large Place Bellecour in the center.

Other Areas: Attractions near the heart of town but out just a little way, such as the intriguing Confluences Museum which is at the bottom of the Presqu'ile.

Simply strolling along the Saône is one of Lyon's great attractions.

---

[7] Traboules and Funiculars are not included in this chapter. These unique attractions, along with silk shops and murals are detailed in following chapters.

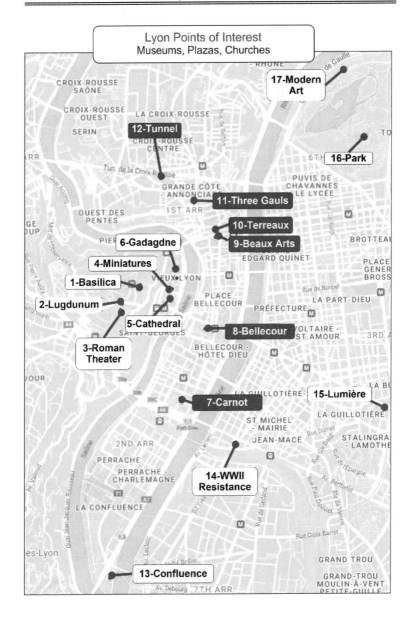

Lyon Points of Interest
Museums, Plazas, Churches

17-Modern Art
12-Tunnel
16-Park
11-Three Gauls
10-Terreaux
6-Gadagdne
9-Beaux Arts
4-Miniatures
1-Basilica
2-Lugdunum
5-Cathedral
8-Bellecour
3-Roman Theater
15-Lumière
7-Carnot
14-WWII Resistance
13-Confluence

Central Lyon Points of Interest List			
Map #	Pg	Type	Name
Vieux Lyon & Fourvière Hill Area			
1	35	Church-Basilica	Basilique Notre Dame de Four-vière
2	38	Roman History	Gallo-Roman Museum-Lugdu-num
3	40	Roman Amphitheater	Théâtre Gallo Roman de Lyon
4	41	Museum-Cinema	Cinema & Miniatures Museum
5	43	Church-Cathedral	Cathédrale Saint-Jean Bap-tiste
6	45	Museum-Multiple	Musée Gadagne, Lyon History & Puppetry Museums
Central & Northern Presqu'île			
7	47	Plaza	Place Carnot
8	48	Plaza	Place Bellecour
9	50	Museum-Art	Museum of Fine Arts/Beaux-Arts
10	52	Plaza & City Hall	Place Terreaux & Hôtel de Ville
11	53	Roman Amphitheater	Amphitheater of the Three Gauls
12	55	Tunnel Attraction	Tunnel de la Croix-Rousse
Attractions Outside of Vieux Lyon or central Presqu'île			
13	56	Museum-Cultural	Confluences Museum
14	59	Museum-WWII	WWII Resistance and Jewish Deportation Museum
15	61	Museum-Cinema	Lumiere Museum
16	62	Park & Zoo	Parc de la Tête d'Or
17	64	Museum-Art	Mac-Lyon-Contemporary Art

Vieux Lyon & Fourvière Points of Interest:

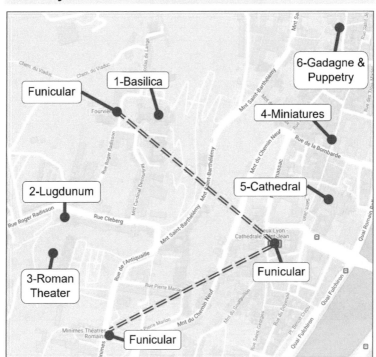

1-Basilique Notre-Dame de Fourvière - Area: Fourvière Hill

It is impossible to miss this building which is a major component of the cityscape. Sitting proudly on top of Fourvière hill, and overlooking Vieux Lyon and the river below, this impressive and beautiful structure looms proudly over the city.

Created near the end of the 19th century, the Basilica Notre-Dame de Fourvière sits on land which was once a Roman forum. This massive structure is a blend of Romanesque and Byzantine architecture. It has four main towers and a bell tower with a gold top.

Locals jokingly refer to this structure as the "upside-down elephant." This is due to the concept of the body resembling an elephant laying on its back with the four towers resembling legs which point up to the sky.

Basilique Notre-Dame de Fourvière

For the first-time visitor to Lyon, this structure and the area surrounding it should be at the top of your list.

- Explore the impressive nave and Saint Thomas chapel
- Numerous mosaics and stained glass
- Visit the crypt of Saint Joseph
- Beautiful views of the city below
- Relax in the Rosary gardens
- Enjoyable travel up to it via a funicular inside the hill
- Climb to the upper towers and rooftop
- Explore neighboring souvenir shops
- The location is an easy stroll to the amphitheater

Cost: There is no entry fee into the basilica. Several different tours are available for a fee and, during the summer season, should be booked in advance. Advanced booking for the tour to the roofs is suggested. Adult rate is 10 Euro or no cost if you have a Lyon City Card

Suggested Duration: Allow a minimum of 2 hours to travel up to the basilica and explore the building and grounds. Three to four hours allows you to include a tour to the towers, enjoy a relaxing lunch and even stroll over to the nearby Roman amphitheater.

Basilique interior

Getting to Here: Three enjoyable methods of traveling up to the basilica from the historical district below are available:

- The funicular. Lyon's funicular system is fun and convenient. You can take a funicular directly from Vieux Lyon, below the basilica. The funicular travels through a tunnel carved in the hill and arrives just a short distance from the basilica entrance.

Roof Tour Notes:

- There is a fee of 10€ for adults.
- Views are incredible.
- You should book in advance during high season.
- Climb 345 stairs.
- The tour takes 90 minutes.

37

- Walk: If you have the ability and time, consider hiking up Fourvière hill to the basilica along a well-marked path.

- Hop-On Bus: The basilica is one stop along the Hop-On, Hop-Off bus route. Consider using this service for ease of transport to/from the top of Fourvière hill to other sights of interest in Lyon.

Further Information: Visit: www.Fourviere.org/en for full details. Tour tickets may be booked on this site.

2-Lugdunum – Gallo Roman Museum of Lyon Fourvière
Area: Fourvière Hill

Lugdunum - Gallo-Roman Museum of Lyon Fourvière
Photo Source: GNRC - Wikimedia Commons

When visiting the large open Roman theater on the hillside overlooking Lyon, be sure to visit the adjoining museum. The "Lugdunum" (the early Roman name for Lyon) or "Gallo-Roman Museum of Lyon Fourvière."

This is an impressive and modern archaeological museum dedicated to Lyon's Roman history and heritage. Visitors are taken to a series of underground chambers called "the exhibition trail" which has the goal of taking visitors back in time.

The museum was built on the grounds on the original site of the ancient city of Ludunum and is tucked discreetly into the hillside so that it is almost invisible from the outside.

Cost: Free entry if you have a Lyon City Card. Otherwise, the adult rate is €4.00 or €7.00 for special exhibits. Tours are also available for a small added fee.

Suggested Duration: Plan on spending 1 hour or more here to view this unique facility.

Web site: Lugdunum.GrandLyon.com.

The Lugdunum is tucked into the hillside next to the Roman Theater

3- Roman Théâtre de Fourvière - Area : Fourvière Hill

Ancient Roman Théâtre de Fourvière
Photo source: Pymouss - Wikimedia Commons

Lyon was an important center of activity for the Romans in France. The presence of three Roman theaters here, attests to this. The largest and most intriguing of these theatres is the Théâtre de Fourvière. This theater is immediately adjacent to the

Odeon theater which was used for smaller events.

The Théâtre de Fourvière was built around 15BC and could hold 10,000 people. When visiting, you may freely explore most of the ruins.

This facility is near the basilica and is less than a five-minute walk. When visiting these ruins, a triangular trip is recommended: (a) take the Fourvière funicular up the hill from Vieux Lyon; (b) walk slightly downhill to the amphitheater, and finally (c) take the Saint-Just funicular line back down to Vieux Lyon. The stop for the Saint-Just funicular is at the bottom of the ruins. You can explore the whole area without having to hike uphill at any point.

Cost: There is no fee to visit these ruins.

Access: In addition to the funicular, (a common method of traveling here), this is a stop for the Hop-On/Hop-Off bus.

4-Cinema & Miniatures Museum - Area: Vieux Lyon

Lyon has a rich history with cinema. Movie making was invented here, and the first public showings of a movie were held here as well. To celebrate this unique heritage, multiple film events are held here each year along with two notable museums which honor this history.

One of many fascinating displays at the Cinema Miniatures Museum

One delightful, small museum which attests to Lyon's cinema history is the Musée Miniature et Cinéma. Nestled on a small cobblestone street in Vieux Lyon, it would be easy to walk on by as there is little in the building's modest exterior to grab your attention and it almost appears to be a tourist trap. It is not.

Visit here if you hold any interest in movie making and, especially, in the art of miniatures and special effects which have been so critical to the visual quality of a good production.

This is a small museum with just 8 display rooms, but those rooms are packed with hundreds of highly detailed miniatures. You will find movie props ranging from costumes, detailed sets, and props from well-known movies such as *Gremlins*, *Spiderman,* and many others.

Cost:[8] Free with Lyon City Card, otherwise…

- Adult rate: €15.90 / Child rate €10.90 (As of October 2023)

When Open: Open every day 10 AM to 6:30 PM

Access: Plan on walking to this museum from almost any point in the historic Vieux Lyon district. It is situated on Rue Saint Jean, immediately across from the large Palais Justice court building. This location is one short block west of the Saône River.

Address: 60 Rue Saint-Jean, 69005, Lyon

Website: www.MuseeMiniatureetCinema.fr

---

[8] Museum of Movie Miniatures Entry Fees: the fees cited for this, and all Lyon area museums are as of mid-2023 and are subject to change.

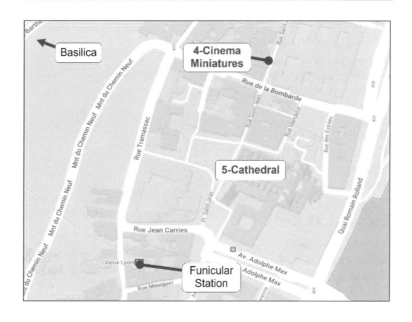

5-Cathédrale Saint-Jean Baptiste - Area: Vieux Lyon

Cathédrale Saint-Jean Baptiste

A surprise to many visitors is to learn that the Cathédrale Saint-Jean Baptiste is far older than the basilica which is perched on the hill just above it.

This cathedral is dedicated to Saint John the Baptist and was completed in 1476, over 500 years ago. It was constructed on the ruins of a previous church built in the 6th century.

The building's exterior is not as impressive as the basilica, but it should not be passed up. Inside are noteworthy treasures including the almost 30-foot-tall astronomical clock.

One of the oldest in Europe, this most-recent version of the clock was installed in 1661.

In addition to the astronomical clock, the 14th century stained-glass windows are beautiful to view. There are 7 panels which depict important Christian events such as the Annunciation, Crucifixion, and Resurrection.

Cost: There is no fee to enter the cathedral.

Location: In the heart of Vieux Lyon, near the Saône River. An easy stroll from anywhere in the historic district.

Astronomical Clock

The Cathedral with the Basilique towering over it from Fourvière hill.
Photo source: Chris 73 - Wikimedia Commons

6-Gadagne Musées[9] / Lyon History[10] and Puppetry Museums
Area: Vieux Lyon

Tucked away on a small street in the historic Vieux Lyon, is Lyon's history museum. This museum is a part of the larger Gadagne Musées, which also includes the unique World Puppetry Museum.

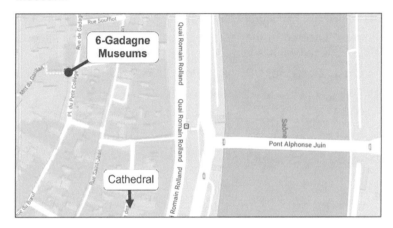

The museums over 80,000 items showcase Lyon's history from its start to present day. Galleries and displays include a wide array of topics ranging from silk history to political and social history. You will find historical objects ranging back to Roman times and the history of Gaul. Included in the 30 display rooms are exhibits of pottery, furniture, and art which highlight the city's history.

The four-floor building surrounds an open courtyard which has hanging gardens on display. Take time to get lunch at the museum's café and enjoy your meal in the courtyard.

---

[9] Hôtel Gadagne: The Gadagne museums are often listed as Hôtel Gadagne – the building the museums are in.

[10] WWII and Resistance Museum. If you are interested in the history of the area, also consider visiting Lyon's WWII and Resistance Museum which is outlined further in this chapter.

Cost: Free with Lyon City Card, otherwise:

- Adult rate: 8€
- Child rate: Free

Suggested Duration: Plan on spending around 2 hours visiting this museum. If time allows, add another hour to enjoy lunch in the outdoor gardens plus a visit to the Puppetry Museum.

When Open: Wednesday through Sunday 10:30 AM to 6 PM.

Access: Located in the historic Vieux Lyon district on Place du Petit Collège which is two blocks from the Saône River.

Address: Gadagne, 1 Place du Petit Collège, 69005 Lyon

Website: www.Gadagne.Musees.Lyon.Fr

Presqu'île Points of Interest:

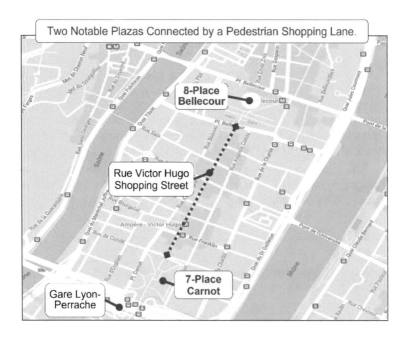

Two Notable Plazas Connected by a Pedestrian Shopping Lane.

8-Place Bellecour

Rue Victor Hugo Shopping Street

7-Place Carnot

Gare Lyon-Perrache

7-Place Carnot - Area: Southern Presqu'île

Place Carnot

Slightly south of Place Bellecour is the large, tree-filled, square Place Carnot. This active park is near the Perrache train station and numerous hotels. Established in the middle of the 19th century, Place Carnot is a place to relax and enjoy a bit of nature in the middle of the city. It was named after a hero of France's revolution.

Take an enjoyable 10-minute walk between Place Carnot and Place Bellecour along Rue Victor-Hugo, a busy pedestrian shopping street filled with a variety of shops and restaurants.

This plaza includes:

- The Statue of the Republique
- Farmer's market every Wednesday afternoon
- Large Christmas market held here
- Children's playground.
- The Catholic University of Lyon borders the park.

8-Place Bellecour - Area: Central Presqu'île

The largest pedestrian square in France, Place Bellecour is at the heart of Lyon's historic district and the Presqu'île. This is an open, nearly tree-less square and a location where many festivals are held each year.

This square is the focus of Lyon's shopping streets. Four avenues lead out from here, including two pedestrian shopping streets. This is also kilometer 0 for Lyon and all distances are measured from here.

Most group tours depart from the Tourist Office which is located here

Place Bellecour
One of the largest open squares in Europe.
Photo source: Google Earth

When visiting here, look for:
- Tourist Office
- Statue of King Louis XIV
- Statue of Saint-Exupéry, the author of *The Little Prince*
- The square is a UNESCO World Heritage Site

- Several times of the year, a large Ferris wheel dominates the center of the plaza.
- Numerous cafes and small restaurants line the streets which border the square.

Location: On Presqu'île, midway both north-to-south and east-to-west on the peninsula.

Access: This large square is an easy walking distance to most attractions, hotels, and museums in the historical area.

- Underground parking available
- Subway, line A – Bellecour stop
- Hop-on/Hop-off bus departs from here.

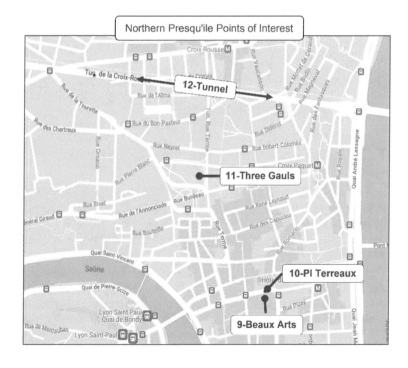

9-Museum of Fine Arts (Musée des Beaux-Arts)

Area: Northern Presqu'île

One of France's largest fine arts collections can be found in Lyon. The Musée des Beaux-Arts de Lyon, built in a former abbey, holds a broad collection of art and artifacts ranging from Egyptian antiquities to current day. Look for major works by Rembrandt, Rubens, Gauguin, Delacroix, and hundreds of others. The Louvre in Paris is the only fine arts museum in France which is larger.

Lyon's Museum of Fine Arts - Musée des Beaux-Arts de Lyon

Located adjacent to the busy Place des Terreaux on Lyon's Presqu'île, this large museum is easy to find and travel to. Immediately upon entering, you are treated to an open, tree-filled courtyard. The numerous galleries surround this inviting and quiet space.

Once inside, 70 rooms may be explored. Museum maps are available at the front desk to help guide you through this large and historic space. Created in 1803, this expansive museum is ranked first among France's regional museums. Among the highlights is the Egyptian collection which covers several rooms.

The paintings collection is impressive by any measure. The focus is on European paintings from the 14th to 20th centuries and they cover 35 rooms of this museum. Look for works by such noted artists as, Van Gogh, Delacroix, Gaugin and Manet among others.

During your visit, take time to enjoy the tearoom and relax on an inviting terrace which opens onto the garden.

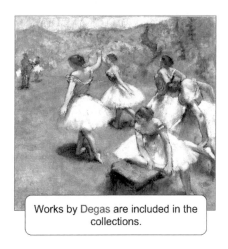

Works by Degas are included in the collections.

Cost: Free with Lyon City Card or Museum Card, or:

- Adult rate = 8€
- Children: free
- Extra charges may apply for temporary exhibitions

When Open: Closed on Tuesdays. Wednesday to Monday from 10 AM to 6 PM.

Suggested Duration: Plan on spending at least 2 or 3 hours here. If your schedule allows, add in some time to enjoy the tearoom for a relaxing break.

Access: Located adjacent to Place des Terreaux and the Hôtel de Ville. If you are staying in central Presqu'île or Vieux Lyon, it is an easy walk to here. Several bus lines stop at Place des Terreaux or take the subway to the Hôtel de Ville stop.

Address: 20 Place des Terreaux, 69001, Lyon

Website: www.MBA-Lyon.fr.

10-Place des Terreaux and the Hôtel de Ville [11]
Area: Northern Presqu'île

This large square is in Lyon's Presqu'île, located less than a mile north of Place Bellecour. The name means "the site of soils", as it was built upon a muddy flat. The plaza is an active hub of activity and is bordered by numerous notable buildings and museums. The history of Place des Terreaux dates to the 12th century and, for centuries, has been the center of local government. It is at the heart of Lyon's 1st Arrondissement and is classified as a World Heritage Site by UNESCO.

Place des Terreaux and the Hôtel de Ville
Photo source: RomainBehar - Wikimedia Commons

The square is scenic and, when viewed at night and fully lit, can be enjoyable to view. Many shops and food stalls can be found here as it is a popular stop for touring groups.

Points of interest here include:

- Hôtel de Ville – Lyons city hall.

---

[11] Hôtel de Ville: In France, buildings with this name are either the current city hall or had previously been the city hall. This is not a hotel.

- Musée des Beaux-Arts
- St. Peter's Palace
- Bartholdi fountain. (The designer of the Statue of Liberty)

Access: This square is an easy walking distance to most attractions and lodgings within the historical district.

- Underground parking available
- Subway lines A & C stop here – Hôtel de Ville stop
- Hop-on/Hop-off bus departs from here.

11-Amphitheater of the Three Gauls:
Area: Northern Presqu'île

Amphitheatre of the Three Gauls
Fourvière Hill and Basilica in the distance

A short walk north from Place Terreaux is another Roman Theater, (In addition to the two noted Roman theaters on Fourvière Hill). It sits in a largely residential and light industry neighborhood and not as large but still is a notable element of Lyon's long history.

This amphitheater was built at the foot of a hill now known as "La Croix-Rousse" and when it was built in 19AD this was the confluence of the Saône and Rhône Rivers. Since then, much of the area now known as Presqu'ile has been modified from a marshy area into the active city it now is.

When it was in active use it was part of a celebration of the area's Gallic tribes and was used for games. It had a capacity of only 1,800 which is quite small when compared to the 10,000-seating capacity of the Theater of Fourvière.

Visiting here does not take a long while as you may only view it from the outside and may not enter the main theater area. There is a path around the theater. The amphitheater sits inside of a small park, the Jardin des Plantes.

Address: Rue Lucien Sportisse, 69001, Lyon

12-Tunnel de la Croix-Rousse - Area: North of Presqu'île

Tunnel de la Croix-Rousse

Step away from the ancient sites and historical monuments and head north to the Tunnel de la Croix-Rousse for something completely different. Safely walk or bicycle through this 1-mile-long tunnel as you marvel at the creative light shows with ambient music which surrounds you the full distance.

Updated in 2013, this tunnel takes you across the Presqu'île from one river to the other. There are parallel tunnels, one for most vehicles d the other for pedestrians, bicycles, and buses. This greatly reduces the number of vehicles and noise you will need to contend with. Once you are in the tunnel, it will take 20 to 25 minutes to walk the full length.

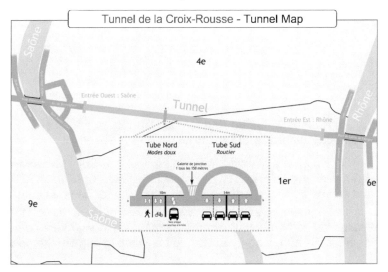

Tunnel de la Croix-Rousse - Tunnel Map

Location: The tunnel is north of Place des Terreaux and the Hôtel de Ville and defines the border between the 1st and 4th arrondissements. It is a 10-minute walk from Terreaux to the Rhône River opening. The Saône River opening is further from the historic district.

Directions: This tunnel is best reached by using Lyon's metro system. You will find convenient stops at both entrances. Bus line C6 and Metro lines A & D access this tunnel.

Cost: There is no fee to visit this unusual attraction.

Attractions On the Edge of Central Lyon

The following 5 Destinations are not in the heart of Presqu'ile and Vieux Lyon areas. In each case, reaching them will require taking local transportation or driving.

(Numbering continues from previously listed points of interest)

13 - Confluence Museum – southern tip of the Presqu'ile

14 - WWII Resistance and Deportation History Centre

15 - Musée Lumière – east of the Presqu'ile

16 - Parc de la Tête d'Or – northeast from the Presqu'ile

17 - Contemporary Art Museum – northeast of Presqu'ile

13-Confluence Museum (Musée des Confluences) :
Area: Southern tip of Presqu'île

Looking like a starship about to take off, the Confluence Museum is an incredible sight. This new facility was opened in 2014 and serves as a science and anthropology center and museum.

The museum is located at the very southern tip of the Presqu'île, at the point where the Saône and Rhône rivers come together. Be sure when you visit, to take time to explore the park area next to the confluence and enjoy the sight of the two historic rivers merging.

Confluence Museum - Musée des Confluences
Photo source: Alexander Baranov - Wikimedia Commons

The mission of the Confluence Museum is different from any other in Lyon and all of Europe. It tells the story of mankind, the history of life, and strives to integrate all of the sciences. When you enter, you are guided through interactive exhibits which take you through time, our history, anthropology, the development of the continents, and life. Collections include items from the stars such as meteorites to ancient fossils.

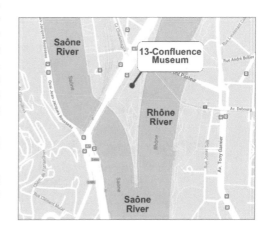

Exhibits are divided into four groupings:

- <u>Origins</u> – from the Big Bang to early societies.

- <u>Species</u> – how humans integrate with the world around them.

- <u>Societies</u> – how cultures and civilizations formed.

- <u>Eternities</u> – differing ways we face the prospect of death and an afterlife.

A museum store and restaurant are on site so consider getting a small meal and enjoying the sight of the rivers flowing by.

Cost: Free with Lyon City Card, or:

- Adults over 25: 9€ (evening rate is reduced)
- Adults 18-25: 5€
- Extra charges may apply for temporary exhibitions

View from the Confluence Museum of the Saône and Rhône coming together.
Photo source: Promethee - Wikimedia Commons

When Open: Closed on Mondays. Typical hours are 10:30AM to 6:30 PM.

Suggested Duration: Plan on spending at least 2 hours here, 3 hours if you will be having a meal during your visit.

Access: Located at the southern tip of the Presqu'île, this is not a destination to consider walking to. If you purchase a Hop-on/Hop-off pass, this stop is included. The light-rail/tram system may be taken from the Perrache train station to the Musée des Confluences rail stop at the end of the line.

Address: 86 Quai Perrache, 69002, Lyon

Website: www.MuseeDesConfluences.fr

14-WWII Resistance and Deportation History Center / Centre d'Histoire de la Résistance et de la Déportation :
Area: Across the Rhône from the Presqu'île

Lyon was an active center of French Resistance against the Germans during WWII. If you visit the traboules (described in chapter 5) many of those were actively used by the resistance movement. This museum is largely dedicated to those silent fighters. The museum also dedicates substantial space to chronicling the unfortunate deportation of Jews from the area.

In a bit of irony, this museum is in a building which had been used by the notorious Gestapo chief Klaus Barbie. It was the site of many tortures of resistance members.

Displays include numerous posters, propaganda items and other memorabilia from this dark period. There are also hundreds of video testimonials from individuals who were made to be part of this.

Cost: Free with Lyon City Card or Museum Card, or the adult rate is 6 Euro.

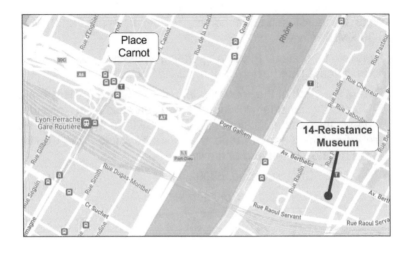

When Open: Closed on Monday and Tuesday. Typical hours are 10 AM to 6 PM.

Access: This is across the Rhône from the Presqu'île, about a 12-to-15-minute walk from Place Carnot. There is a tram stop just one block away. Take the T2 line to the Centre-Berthelot-Sciences tram stop.

Address: 14 avenue Berthelot, 69007 Lyon

Website: chrd.lyon.fr

15-Museum Lumière - Area: East from the Presqu'île

Musée Lumière
Where cinema was invented

The Musée Lumière is the site where movies and cinematography were born. Come to the home of the Lumière Brothers, the individuals who are credited as the fathers of cinema. Their family home is now a museum honoring their invention and the early history of film.

This museum which just completed a major renovation in mid-2023 is dedicated to the preservation of French film making. Inside, you can visit displays of some of the earliest equipment used in film making and watch showings of the earliest movies ever produced. There are inter-active exhibits on four floors.

Cost: Free with Lyon City Card, or: Adult rate: 8€. Child and senior rate: 7€.

Suggested Duration: Plan on spending around 1 hour visiting this museum.

Facilities: There is a café and bookshop on site, also an elevator for use by mobility-impaired individuals.

Access: The museum is in the 8th arrondissement, approximately 2 miles east of the historical district. For most visitors to Lyon, the best way to travel here is to take the subway. Use line D and get off at the Monplaisir-Lumière stop. From there, it is a short 1-block walk. When here, take time to enjoy Place Ambroise Courtois, a large open park across the street from the museum.

Address: 25 Rue du Premier Film, 69008, Lyon.

Website: www.Institut-Lumiere.org

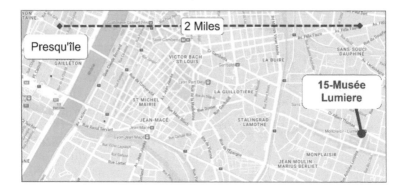

16-Parc de la Tête d'Or
Area: Slightly northeast from the Presqu'ile

Parc de Tête d'Or
Photo source: Simlaurent - Wikipedia

This large urban park is slightly north and outside Lyon's historical area. Located along the Rhône River, in the 6th arrondissement, the park is well worth a visit on a nice day.

The Parc de Tête d'Or (Park of the Golden Head) is over 290 acres in size. It is also adjacent to the large Contemporary Art Museum which allows visitors to combine two different experiences.

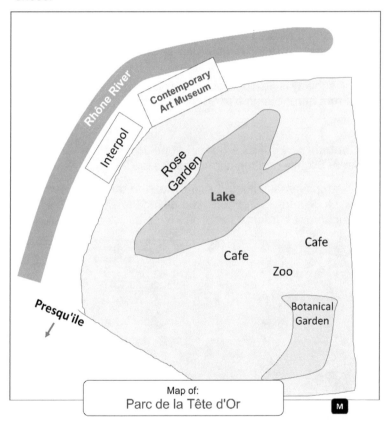

Map of:
Parc de la Tête d'Or

The park includes attractions for young and old:
- Large lake – peddle boat rentals available
- Numerous trails for walking, jogging, or bicycling
- Expansive rose garden with large greenhouses

- Playgrounds
- Lyon's zoo
- Multiple cafés
- Miniature train encircles the park

Cost: Entrance is free.

Directions: Unless you are staying near this park, most individuals will find Lyon's bus system to be the most convenient method. Several bus lines stop here, so directions will vary based on your starting point. A detailed bus map is available from the Tourist Office.

The subway is also available. The closest stop is Masséna station. From here, it is an 8 to 10-minute walk to the park.

17-Contemporary Arts Museum / Musée d'art Contemporain
Area: Slightly northeast from the Presqu'île

This museum is situated slightly next to the large Parc de la Tête d'Or. When visiting here, you never know what you will find as it undergoes frequent and nearly complete transformations.

Contemporary Arts Museum
Musée d'art Contemporain

Most of what is here is temporary. As a result, there are frequent and lengthy closures which occur each time it is undergoing a transformation.

Come here for the unusual and unexpected. To get a taste of what you will find here, go to the museum's website at: www.Mac-Lyon.com. Once you are on the museum's website, visit the page which provides virtual tours of past exhibits.

When visiting here, consider combining this experience with an afternoon in the expansive Parc de la Tête d'Or.

A café and bookshop are on the property in addition to the facility's proximity to both a large Marriott Hotel and a Crowne Plaza, both of which have full-service restaurants.

Cost: Free with Lyon City Card, the Museum Card, or:

- Adults over 25: 9€ (Euro)
- Adults 18-25: 6€
- Children: free

When Open: Check the website's schedule to determine current hours. As cited earlier, this facility is occasionally closed to facilitate changing exhibitions. Normal hours are Wednesday to Sunday from 11 AM to 6 PM, Closed Monday and Tuesday.

Access: City buses are your best option. Take lines C1 or C4 and get off at the Musée d'art Contemporain stop. There is no nearby access to tram or subway lines.

Address: Cité Internationale, 81 Quai Charles de Gaulle, 69006 Lyon

Website: www.Mac-Lyon.com

5: Traboules, Bouchons, Silk & Murals
Lyon's Unique Treasures

Lyon offers visitors several unique experiences. Even if you are in the city for a short visit, putting these delights at the top of your list of sights to visit should be considered. Each of the four treats listed here will give you something which cannot be found elsewhere.

- Traboules: An informal network of elusive passageways throughout the historic area.

- Bouchons: In a city known for its cuisine, these small family-owned specialty restaurants stand out.

- Silk: Visit historic silk shops, watch it being made and take-home unique silk items found nowhere else.

- Murals: View some of Europe's largest and most intricate out-door murals as you wander through the historic district.

Traboules: A fun way to directly experience some of Lyon's history is to explore the secret passageways called Traboules. As many as 500 of these intriguing, covered hallways exist, with less than 80 open to the public. The word Traboule is a derivation of a Latin phrase which means to pass through. The oldest of these dates to the 4th century and was created to allow direct access to the rivers without having to work your way through the town's twisting network of streets.

Some History: These passageways grew in importance as Lyon's silk industry grew. They enabled workers to transport the precious textiles while staying out of the weather. During the height of the silk trade, in the early 1800s, there were over 20,000 silk workers in Lyon and their usage of the Traboules was critical in the growth of this industry.

You can pick up a Traboules Map at the Lyon Tourism Office on Place Bellecour.

During WWII, the French Resistance was able to use these passageways to meet secretly and spy on the Nazis. The Nazis were prevented from completely taking over the city in part because of this initiative.

Inside a Traboule: The traboules are little more than hallways which provide shortcuts from one of Lyon's narrow streets to another. At times, these hallways are simple, straight affairs. Others seem to twist and wind their way between buildings. They are almost always covered with only a few openings to provide light.

The purpose for exploring the traboules is not to experience something grand or intricate. Explore these passages to experience a unique chapter of history and imagine yourself as a silk worker scurrying from one part of town to another. Or think of yourself hiding from the Nazis and watching their movements.

Finding Traboules:[12] It is easy to walk by a traboule entrance and not know it is there. For the 80 which are open to the public only a few are marked. The marked traboule etrances

Inside one of Lyon's hidden Traboules

---

[12] Traboules App for Apple: An interactive app, "Traboules by Lyon Tourism" is available in the Apple store. Unfortunately, as of this writing in mid-2023, this app is not also available via the Google / Android Play Store.

have symbols on building walls near them (see photo below). Without knowledge of these symbols, it is unlikely you would know a traboule exists as the doorways are purposefully plain in appearance. One caution, during high season, the more popular traboules can be crowded with tour groups.

Traboule Symbols on Buildings

Most Traboules are in two areas of town:

- Vieux Lyon – by far the best area to explore traboules and there are nearly 200 of them here. Some of the best passages/traboules to visit are here and several are in close proximity to one another. Another bit of good news is most of these are easy to find. See the following table for a list of the of the more popular traboules.

- Croix-Rousse - North of Place Terreaux: The second-best area for exploring traboules is just a short distance north of Place Terreaux on the Presqu'île.

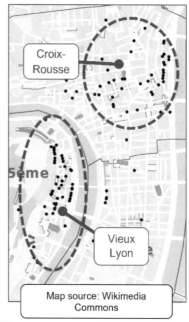

Map source: Wikimedia Commons

68

It is formally known as Croix-Rousse. There are nearly 160 traboules in the area and one of the better-known ones, the "Traboule de la Cour des Voraces" is a popular destination. This area is where having the interactive app or a map from the Tourist Office in hand really helps.

Locations of Some of the More Notable Traboules (All recommended Traboules are in Vieux Lyon)	
Start & End	Where to Find
2 Pl du Gourvernement 10 quai Romain Rolland	Look for the small street "Rue Saint-Jean" The traboule leads off from a small plaza which is roughly 2 blocks north off the large Palace of Justice.
27 rue Saint-Jean 6 rue des Trois-Maries	One block north of the Cinema Miniatures Museum -on the opposite site of the street.
54 rue Saint-Jean 27 rue du Boeuf	The longest traboule and possibly the most photographed. Easy to find from rue Saint-Jean, ½ block north from Rue du Palais de Justice.
10 et 12 rue St-Georges 5 Place Neuve St. Jean	A three block walk southwest from the funicular station.

Guided Traboule Tours: Several walking tours of historic Lyon are available and most of these tours include explorations of the most notable traboules. Check with Lyon's Tourist Office for details.

Bouchons: Like so much else in Lyon, the unique, small restaurants known as bouchons, have a direct link to the earlier silk trade. During the 19th century, silk weavers would visit these inexpensive establishments after work to enjoy a pot of Lyonnais' pork or fish with some local wine. The tradition and nature of these small restaurants has continued to the current day.

The fare in these restaurants was created for individuals with little money. The cuts of meat were from the lowest cuts of fish, poultry, and pork. The restaurateurs learned to be creative with the least desirable elements and this evolved into a unique set of dishes which are found nowhere else. The quality has evolved and improved dramatically although be prepared for some unusual dishes.

Most bouchons will be identified with the term "Bouchon Lyonnais"
Photo source: Peter Glyn-Wikimedia Commons

The term Bouchon, essentially means twigs. The bouchon owners would simply hang a bunch of small sticks at the door to advertise their existence.

Bouchons and bistros are similar. One of the biggest differences is that bouchons have a far more limited menu than bistros.

Official bouchons, those recognized by Lyon's Chamber of Commerce, will have the logo cited here hanging outside. They also are the only establishments authorized to use the term Bouchon Lyonnais. This name and emblem help to avoid confusion as many bistros use the term bouchon even if they do not have the historical bouchon roots.

Bouchon Interior
Bouchon Lyonnais Le Caveau Des Gourmands
Located on the Presqu'île near Place des Terreaux

The fare offered here is limited and the number of tables and seats are often limited as well. Be prepared to find creative cuisine which you will not encounter anywhere else. Most bouchons are not open every day so pay attention to their schedule. Dinner hours tend to not start until 7 PM for most locations. You will also find that they are generally closed after lunch, leaving the family and staff time to enjoy an afternoon siesta.

Locations of Bouchons: Bouchons are distributed in areas that roughly coincide with the same sections of town where most traboules are. Many of the more notable bouchons will be found on

either Vieux Lyon or Croix-Rousse area in the first arrondissement.

Area	Bouchon Name	Address	Days Open
Bouchons to Consider [13]			
Area: VL=Vieux Lyon // NP=Presquîle, north of Place Bellecour // SP= Presquîle, south of Place Bellecour			
VL	Les Fines Gueules	16 Rue Lainerie	Tu to Sat[14]
	Daniel et Denis Saint-Jean	36 rue Tramassac	Tu to Sat
	Au Comptoir Les Gones	34 Rue Saint Jean	Daily
	Aux Trois Maries	1 Rue des Trois-Maries	Tu-Sun
	Les Lyonnais	19 Rue de la Bombarde	Tu to Sun
	Le Laurencin	24 rue Saint-Jean	Daily
NP	Le Bouchon des Cordeliers	15 rue Claudia	Tu to Sat
	Le Bistrot d'Abel (Author favorite)	47 rue de la Bourse	Tu to Sat
	L'Acteur	5 rue Charles Dullin	Tu to Sat
	Les Culottes Longues	42 re Sala	Tu to Sat

[13] Listed Bouchons: This is a sample listing only. Full details relating to their cuisine and character may be found on sites such as TheFork.com (Then search for Lyon Bouchons)

[14] Bouchon Hours & Days: It is common for these small restaurants to be open in two segments during the day. Typically, they will be open for lunch and then close until around 7 PM to again open for dinner. Most family-fun bouchons are closed on Sunday and Monday.

Bouchons to Consider [13]			
Area: VL=Vieux Lyon // NP=Presquîle, north of Place Bellecour // SP= Presquîle, south of Place Bellecour			
Area	Bouchon Name	Address	Days Open
	La Mere Lea	11 quai des Célestins	M to Sat
	Café des Federations	9 rue Major Martin	Daily
SP	Le Poêlon d'Or	29 rue des Ramparts d'Ainay	M to Sat
	Le Vivarais	1 place Galleton	Tu to Sat
	Café Comptoir Abel	25 rue Guynemer	Daily

Silk Stores and Workshops: The making of silk was a large part of Lyon's history, and it comes as no surprise that many silk shops exist today. The silk shops in Lyon range from small, historic workshops to large galleries which largely cater to tourists. The world's finest silk goods may be found here and is often used in museums. Expect to

Silk Saint-Georges

find silk of the highest quality here, along with some notable prices.

Quality silk shops may be found throughout the historic district with the oldest being in Vieux Lyon.[15] One workshop, Silk Saint-Georges, stands above the rest for the experience it provides.

Silk Saint-Georges: [16] This small shop is tucked away in Vieux Lyon. Come here to view silk being made in the workshop which uses some of Lyon's oldest looms. Live demonstrations are often conducted. The breadth of wares offered is small, but the quality and the experience make the visit worthwhile.

Silk Saint-Georges, Soierie Saint-Georges, is on a small street a short walk uphill from the funicular station. The address is: 11 rue Mourget.

Interior of Silk Saint-Georges
The store has an active silk workshop which may be explored.

---

[15] Silk Shop Directory: Many of the better stores may be found described on the following website. En.VisiterLyon.com – when on the home page, search for "Silk Fashion."

[16] Silk Saint-Georges: This store/museum/workshop is classified in some guidebooks as a museum and not a store. It is both.

Notable Vieux Lyon & Presqu'île Silk Shops: After you visit the historic Silk Saint-Georges and are still looking for high quality silk products made in Lyon, the following stores should be considered. There are other notable silk shops, even a small museum, but the stores listed here are the most central and convenient.

> Soieries
> This is the French word for silks.

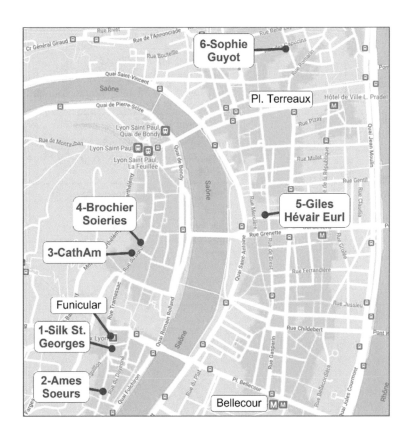

Silk Shops to Explore		
Map #	Name	Details
1	Silk Saint Georges	11 Rue Mourget – Vieux Lyon www.SoieriesSaintGeorges.com Historic small silk shop and factory.
2	Ames Soeurs	29 Rue Saint-Georges – Vieux Lyon www.AmesSoeurs-Edition.com Upscale, artistic silks.
3	CathAm Soie	24 Rue du Bœuf - Vieux Lyon www.Catham-Soie.com Family-run silk fashion house founded by a Parisian stylist.
4	Brochier Soieries	16 Rue du Boeuf – Vieux Lyon www.Soierie-Lyonnnaise.com Family-owned silk workshop since the 1950s.
5	Giles Hévair Eurl	14 Rue de Brest – Presqu'île www.Giles-Hevair.com Silk boutique with a focus on scarves and bow ties.
6	Sophie Guyot Soies	8 Rue Saint-Polycarpe – Presqu'île www.SophieGuyot.com Upscale silk store and workshop.

Murals: Scattered throughout Lyon are more than 100 large and impressive wall murals/frescos. The central theme of these murals is to depict the city's history. Dozens of artists and architects have steadily worked on this project for over forty years.

"Wall of the Canuts" / "Mur des Canuts"
Mural located in the 4th arrondissement

To view all of the larger murals would have you traveling throughout the city and its suburbs. Luckily, several of the more notable murals are found in the 1st and 4th arrondissements, the area just north of Place des Terreaux.

If you choose to ride the Hop-on/Hop-Off bus, the tour stops at some of the larger murals along the route. This can be helpful as several of them are well outside the area most visitors would normally be walking through.

Location of some notable Historic District Murals:

- "Wall of the Canuts" – rue Denfert Rochereau – 4th arr.

- "The Silk Roads" – 4 rue Carguillat, Clos Jouve – 1st arr.

- "Famous Faces of Lyon" – 2 rue de la Martinière – 1st arr.

- "The City Library" – 6 rue de la Platière – 1st arr.

6: Getting Around in Lyon

Walking, Trams, Hop-On Bus & Funiculars

Lyon's historic and tourist center is easy to navigate and many of the leading attractions are near one another. Rental cars are not needed and most of your explorations may be done by walking or taking one of the convenient trams, the subway, or Hop-on/Hop-Off buses. One of the few times you may want to take a taxi would be to travel to or from the airport.

Walking:[17] Most visitors stay in Lyon's Presqu'île or Vieux Lyon sectors. By staying in these areas of town, almost every leading attraction can be reached by a short, pleasant walk.

If you are in the mood to shop, the Rue de la République is a noted pedestrian shopping street which stretches over several blocks in the Presqu'ile. This was the first street in France to become a pedestrian-only street. Along here, there are shops and restaurants ranging from small boutiques to upscale department stores. One end of this avenue may be found at Place Bellecour with the other at the Hôtel de Ville.

> **Caution**
>
> Vieux Lyon is steep in some areas and there are cobblestones which can be problematic for mobility impaired individuals.

---

[17] Walking Directions and Map App: Download the Lyon Map and Walks app by GPS My City.

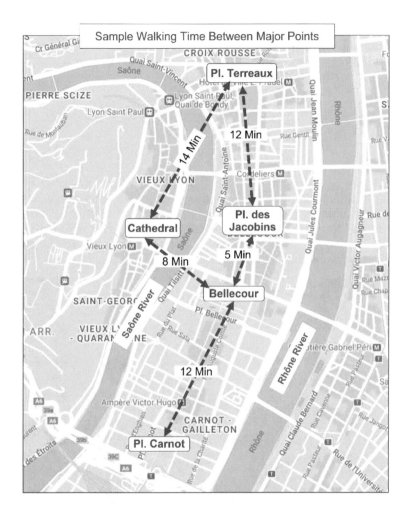

Sample Walking Time Between Major Points

Attractions/areas not recommended to walk to: These areas are NOT easy to reach on foot.

- Top of Fourvière Hill. The impressive Basilica Notre Dame de Fourvière and the Roman theater are here. This hilltop location is best reached by taking one of the enjoyable funiculars from Vieux Lyon at the foot of the hill.

- <u>Confluence Museum</u>. This modern museum is at the southern tip of the Presqu'île and not easy to reach on foot. The best way to travel to this museum is to either ride the Hop-On/Hop-Off bus or take the tram from Gare de Lyon Perrache.

Funiculars: One of the more enjoyable ways to travel in Lyon is to ride the funiculars to the top of Fourvière Hill which is 300 feet above Vieux Lyon. These are small red tram-like cars which travel from Vieux Lyon up the hill to your choice of the basilica or the Roman amphitheater.

Lyon's Funiculars
Two routes starting from the same point in Vieux Lyon.

The cost is 3,50€ per person for a round-trip ticket as of mid-2023 OR if you have a Lyon City Card, the ride is included.

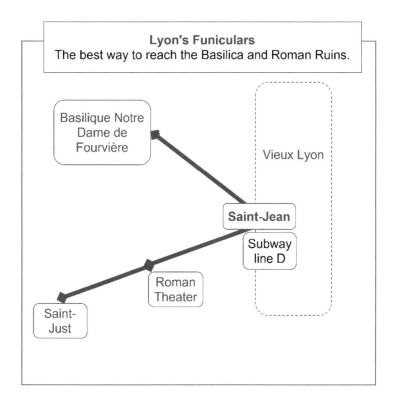

Lyon's Funiculars
The best way to reach the Basilica and Roman Ruins.

Basilique Notre Dame de Fourvière

Vieux Lyon

Saint-Jean

Subway line D

Roman Theater

Saint-Just

When riding the funiculars, much of the trip is underground. The trip to the basilica also lets you out at an underground station, just a few feet from the basilica's entrance.

The trip to the Roman amphitheaters lets you out in a spot which is a short walk to the bottom of the amphitheater. The name of the tram stop for the roman theaters is "Minimes Thèâtre Romains".

Hop-On/Hop-Off Bus Tour: [18] Hop-On/Hop-Off bus tours can be found in most cities which attract tourism and Lyon is no exception. It is easy to think of this service as excessively touristy, but these bus tours do offer several benefits.

Lyon's Hop-On/Hop-Off Bus / City Tour

Several attractions are not within easy walking distance and often it is easy to walk right by buildings or plazas with historical significance without knowing what you are missing. These tour buses will take you to most leading points of interest, including several, such as the Confluence Museum, which are out of the way. They also allow you to get off and on at your leisure.

Full details on this program including ticket purchase may be found at www.LyonCityTour.fr (and other resellers such as Vistor.com).

---

[18] Hop-On Tour Blue Line: In addition to the primary "Green Line" described here, another route, the "Blue Line" may also be available. As of this writing, this second route had been suspended so no details on it are provided here.

If you have a Lyon City Card, the rates for these tours are reduced.

Some Details:

- The City Tour's green route makes 12 stops and the total ride, (if taken without getting off along the route) is 1 hour and 45 minutes.

- The starting point is at Place Bellecour (the plaza which has the Tourist Office) but you may get on and start your journey at any of the stops.

- Notable stops for this route include Vieux Lyon, the Confluences, Place des Terreaux, Fourvière Hill and the Gallo-Roman theater.

- This tour bus runs roughly every 40 minutes to a full hour depending on the season and day you are there.

- The full rate for a one-day ticket is 22€ (As of late 2023) for adults or 9€ for children. City Card discounts the rate 2 Euro. Other group and family ticket packs are available as well.

.

Subways and Trams: Lyon has a convenient combination of

subways and trams which enable visitors to easily move around the city. This is not a complex system and is easy to learn which line to take and what is required to board. The map on the following page shows the lines which visitors are most likely to use.

On the Presqu'île, there is one north-south line which provides visitors easy travel from the Hôtel de Ville in the north to Place Carnot and the Perrache train station in the south.

Subway stops, listed on the next page, on the Presqu'île are limited so some knowledge of where the stops can be helpful.

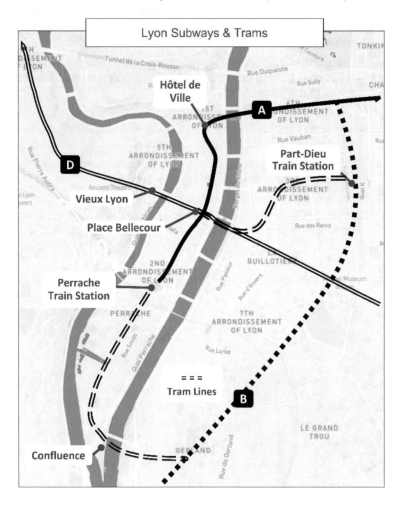

Presqu'île Subway stops – Line A:

- <u>Hôtel de Ville</u>: Use this stop for the Beaux Arts Museum and Place des Terreaux.

- <u>Cordeliers:</u> Midway between Hôtel de Ville and Place Bellecour. Use this stop to tour the popular pedestrian shopping street Rue de la Republique.

- <u>Place Bellecour</u>: The location of the Tourist Office and jumping-off point for most tours.

- <u>Ampère–Victor Hugo</u>: Midway between Place Bellecour and Gare Perrache. Getting off here will take you to another pedestrian shopping street, Rue Victor Hugo. At this point, you are just a three-block walk to Place Carnot.

- <u>Gare Perrache</u>. This is the southern point of Line A of the subway where you come out under the busy train station. Getting off here will allow you to easily catch the tram to the Confluence.

> Lyon City Cards cover the cost of subways, trams, and the funiculars. No additional purchase is required.
>
> Go to one of the sales offices to acquire a ticket which is covered by the City Card.

<u>Subway and Tram System Map:</u> You can pick up a detailed map at the Tourist Office or online. [19] These maps are also often found posted on signs in major locations such as Lyon's train station. Most of Lyon's tram stations have convenient maps posted which will provide the information you need.

> Lyon Metro Website The official website for Lyon transportation is www.TCL.fr.

Cost: (As of Mar-2023)

- One-hour ticket: 2€

---

[19] Subway and Tram map online: Check www.MetroEasy.com then select Lyon from the menu of cities to view and download a detailed map of Lyon's system.

- 24-hour pass 3,5€
- Book of 10 tickets 19 €

Purchasing Tickets: If you do not have a Lyon City Card, you will need to purchase tickets to ride any mode of public transportation in Lyon. There is no need to purchase these tickets in advance or online. Simply go to any bus, tram, funicular or subway stop and ticket machines will be available. Both cash and credit cards may be used, and English is a language option.

A subway station in Lyon.
Photo source: Florian Fèvre - Wikipedia

Bicycle Rental: Much of Lyon can easily be explored on bicycle and with a large network of bike trails and routes, it is easy to do so. Lyon's bicycle program is the second largest in France.

There are over 340 self-serve Vélo'v Bicycle Rental stations in Lyon.
Photo source: Google Maps

There are several firms which provide bicycle and e-bike rentals. By far, the largest service is Vélo'v, with over 340 self-serve stations throughout Lyon.

To rent a bicycle from this service, either use the app or the rental kiosk at each station. Bikes may be returned to any station with available docking stations.

There are several available rates. A one-day rental is 4 Euro and bikes may be rented for any period desired.

Website: Velov.GrandLyon.com

> **Vélo'v App**
> Download and use the app to locate rental stations and rent bikes.

~ ~ ~ ~ ~ ~

If you will be staying in Lyon for several days and participating in several activities or tours in this city, you should consider purchasing a "Lyon City Card." There is also a Museum Card available, but the Lyon City Card provides broader benefits.

Lyon City Card: These passes provide value and convenience IF you plan on visiting multiple museums or similar attractions. They are fairly expensive so do not purchase one if you will be spending your time outside the city, exploring parks or just shopping and strolling.

> The Lyon City Card is available for 1, 2, 3 or 4 days.

The passes provide a mix of free and discounted attractions. See the following pages for details.

The City Cards may be purchased from the main Tourist Office at Place Bellecour. You may also purchase city passes online prior to visiting Lyon. They may be purchased from several online sources including:

- www.LyonCityCard.com
- www.Viator.com
- www.GetYourGuide.com

Allow two weeks for the print version of passes to be mailed to you once you purchase them online.

Prices: As of late-2023, the full, non-discounted rates per adult for the passes were as shown on the next page. Discounts may be available if purchased in advance online.[20]

> Visit:
>
> www.LyonCityCard.com for full, updated, details on the City Cards.

- 1 Day Pass = 29€
- 2 Day Pass = 39€ (Avg of: 19.50 Euro per day)
- 3 Day Pass = 49€ (Avg of 16,30 Euro per day)
- 4 Day Pass = 59€ (Avg of 14.75 Euro per day)

Some of What Is Included in the Lyon City Card fare: [21]

Saône River Cruise - Included in the Lyon City Card

---

[20] City Card Price Information is from: www.LyonCityCard.com. Rates for students and children are less. No rates for seniors are quoted on this site. Rates may be more on 3rd party providers such as Viator.com. An additional rate-band includes airport transportation.

[21] Lyon City Card inclusions: This guide depicts many of the more notable sights included within the City Card. Not all tours and attractions are shown here as the list can and does change. Check www.LyonCityCard.com for an updated list.

- Transportation: Unlimited use of Lyon's subways, trams, and funiculars. Soane river cruise.

- Guided Tours: Discounted admission to the Lyon Hop-On Bus, Aquarium, and Lyon City Tram (An open-air small tram tour of Croix-Rousse area).

- Shopping: Discounts and coupons for many of Lyon's shops.

- Museums and monuments: Most museums are included.
  - Confluence Museum
  - Beaux-Arts/Fine Arts Museum
  - Museum of Modern Art
  - Cinema and Miniature Museum
  - Tissue/Textiles and Decorative Arts Museum

> Over 80 attractions are included in the card. Most are free with the card, some are discounted.

Lyon Croix-Rousse Tram Tours
Photo Courtesy of LyonCityTour.fr

Museum Card: This pass is more intended for local citizens as, once it is purchased, it is good for a full year. Once a pass is purchased, it provides unlimited visits to each museum.

Six museums are included in this pass including the Museum of Fine Arts, Printing Museum and Gadgne Museum, and Resistance Museum.

Additional museums such as the Confluence Museum provide discounts to holders of the Museum Card.

Cost: The annual adult rate as of late 2023 is 25 Euro. These passes should be purchased at the reception desk of each participating museum.

Lyon City Tour Companies: If your schedule allows, consider taking one of the many tours within Lyon. These tours range from short 1-or-2-hour events to full day explorations.

Even if you are disinclined to join structured group events, at least one tour should be considered as they almost always enhance your understanding of the city, its history, and main attractions.

Most tours of interest will be available from the Tourist Office, and many may be purchased in advance.

Numerous online services enable you to explore available tours and purchase passes. These offerings often go well beyond those offered by the Tourist Office and some tours may be customized to your specifications.

Some of the leading tour providers are:

- En.VisiterLyon.com – Lyon Tourist Office
- TripAdvisor.com – search for Lyon and go to the tours page
- Viator.com (A service of Trip Advisor)
- GetYourGuide.com – search for Lyon to view the provided tours.
- ToursByLocals.com (This firm offers many private and small-group tours)

Example Lyon City Tours: The following tables outline several recommended tours. Each of these may be purchased from the Lyon Tourist Office. Many other tours are available through other companies such as those cited above. The Tourist Office is a great place to  start your search for tours as they offer a full variety ranging from walking, historic, gastronomic, historical, and even whimsical tour offerings.

- Vieux Lyon Walking Tour – 2 hours to historical highlights within the historic Vieux Lyon sector or Lyon.

- Croix-Rousse City Tram – 1 hour ride in an open-air tram through the area north of the Presqu'ile. The tour starts near the Place des Terreaux. (Included in the Lyon City Card)

- Traboules Walking Tour – A small group tour to several of the intriguing traboules in Vieux Lyon. The tour lasts 1 hour.

- Lyon Food Tour – Lyon is known for its cuisine and this walking tour shows you why. A 2-hour tour in central Lyon, starting from Place Bellecour and includes several tastings.

- Saône River Cruise – One of several boat tours available on Lyon's rivers. A relaxing 1-hour ride on a two-deck boat with narrative. Board at a dock on the Saône River at the foot of the Palais de Justice Bridge.

- Gourmet Walking Tour – One of several helpful food tours in historic Lyon. This 3-hour tour focuses on area delicacies specific to Lyon and includes several tastings. It departs from the Lyon Opera House near the Hôtel de Ville at Place Terreaux.

The above list is only a sample of available tours which will help you become acquainted with Lyon. All of the above are provided by the Lyon Tourist Office but similar offerings may be found from other leading tour providers such as Viator or Get Your Guide, and others.

~ ~ ~ ~ ~ ~

8: Where to Stay in Lyon

Quality lodging may be found throughout Lyon but determining where to stay as a first-time visitor need not be complicated. This guide outlines four areas to consider booking your lodging. In each case, these sections of town provide easy access to main sights, transportation, shopping and dining.

Recommendation:

Stay near Place Bellecour or Place des Jacobins for your first visit.

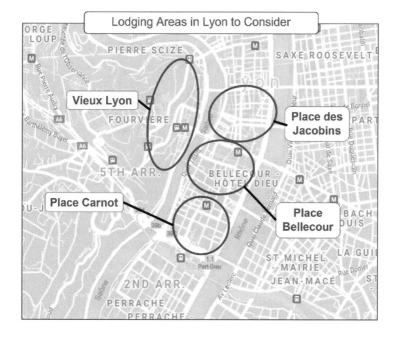

Lodging Areas in Lyon to Consider

Other areas are not detailed here simply because they are not as central to these four. In addition, the focus of this guide is on hotels and not apartment rentals such as Air B & B. When considering lodging, using a source such as TripAdvisor.com or Booking.com is recommended as they can provide far more detail and up-to-date reviews.

Place des Jacobins: Situated conveniently between Place Bellecour and Place des Terreaux, is the small but historic Place des Jacobins. The square and the lodging here is midway between the Saône and Rhône rivers.

Place des Jacobins
Photo source: Tiana Rakoto - Wikimedia Commons

Positives of staying near Place des Jacobins: This area is ideal for travelers to Lyon who are seeking convenient, boutique and midsize hotels. These are just steps from numerous restaurants and shops and only a short walk to many historic sights.

Another plus is this is not an excessively busy neighborhood and no major thoroughfares run through here.

Numerous restaurants line the streets and the major shopping areas are close by including the popular pedestrian shopping street Rue de la Republique.

This location is a short 5-minute walk to Place Bellecour where the Tourist Office is and where many tours depart. To the west, it is less than a 10-minute walk across the Saône to the heart of Vieux Lyon.

Hotels in this area are a short walk to major landmarks and points of interest including both rivers, Place Bellecour, Cathédrale Saint-Anne, and the Quinconces Plaza where the Tourist Office is located and where most tours depart.

Negatives of staying near Place des Jacobins: Negatives of staying in this area are few. The subway does not stop here, so to ride the subway you must walk roughly 5 minutes to the nearest stop. The only other negative, a common one across most areas in a city, is the lack of noteworthy views.

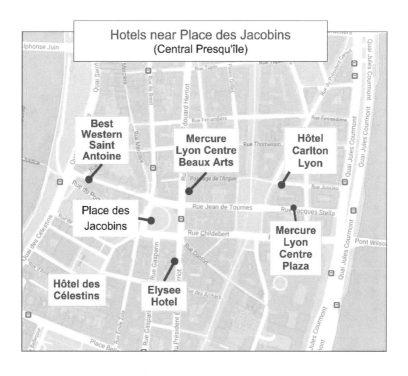

Hotels near Place des Jacobins
(Central Presqu'île)

Properties to consider near Place des Jacobins		
Hotel Name	Rating	Website
Best Western Saint Antoine	3.5	www.BestWestern.com Then search for Lyon.
Elysée Hotel	3	www.HotelElysee.fr
Hôtel Carlton Lyon	4.5	www.Hotel-Carlton-Lyon.com
Hôtel des Célestins	3	www.HotelCelestins.com
Mercure Lyon Centre Beaux-Arts	4	www.Mercure.Accor.com
Mercure Lyon Centre Plaza République	4 [22]	Note – this is a large chain with several properties with similar names.

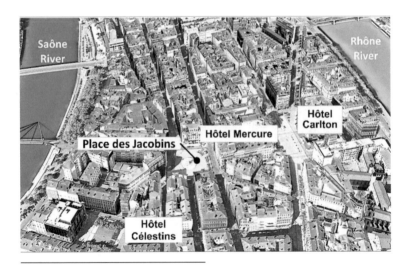

Saône River

Rhône River

Hôtel Carlton

Hôtel Mercure

Place des Jacobins

Hôtel Célestins

---

[22] Hotel Ratings. All ratings cited in this guide are a combination of author's experiences and other user reviews. No one single source is used.

Place Bellecour Area: Place Bellecour is about as central as you can get. This is officially "kilometer 0" for Lyon and all distances are measured from here. Numerous hotels, small and large, are near this large plaza and you can find lodging ranging from budget to luxury.

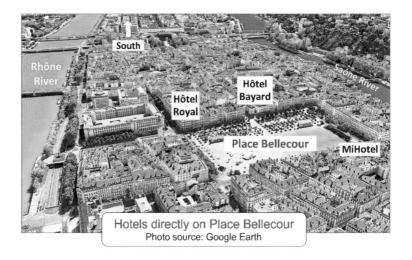

Hotels directly on Place Bellecour
Photo source: Google Earth

Positives of staying near Place Bellecour: This area is very central, a short walk to many landmarks, and to both the Rhône and Saône Rivers. For transportation, subways lines stop at Place Bellecour, and you can catch lines going in any direction. Catching a subway from here to either of the main train stations is easy to do.

If you are planning on taking any day trips or tours of the area, most of these depart from the Tourist Office which is in Place Bellecour.

Numerous restaurants may be found here, especially if you visit the delightful, and somewhat hidden, Rue des Marronniers pedestrian street which is just ½ block east from Place Bellecour.

Negatives of staying near Place Bellecour: Negatives of staying here are few. The biggest problem (which is seasonal) is the noise levels from Place Bellecour. Many festivals are held in this large plaza and noise from these events can be an unwelcome factor. The good news is this is largely mitigated by the hotels having soundproof windows.

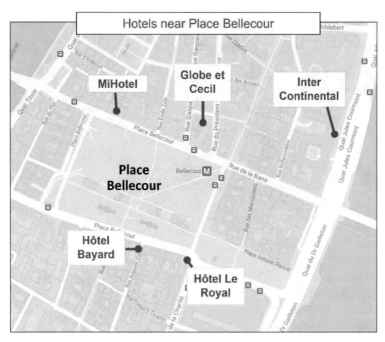

Hotels near Place Bellecour

Properties to consider near Place Bellecour		
Hotel Name	Rating	Website
Globe et Cecil	4	www.GlobeEtCecilHotel.com
Hôtel Bayard Bellecour	3.5	www.HotelBayard.fr

Properties to consider near Place Bellecour		
Hotel Name	Rating	Website
Hotel Royal / Hôtel le Royal Lyon	4.5	www.LyonHotel-LeRoyal.com
InterContinental Lyon Hotel Dieu	4.5	www.Intercontinental.com Then search for Lyon.
MiHotel	4	www.MiHotel.fr Note: There is more than 1 Mi-Hotel in Lyon. Another property is across the river in Vieux Lyon.

Vieux Lyon Area: The Vieux Lyon historic area is filled with many small restaurants/bouchons, historic sights and shops, all nestled amid a maze of narrow cobble streets. Lodging here ranges from small and boutique inns to upscale lodging such as the Villa

Villa Florentine
Upscale hotel in Vieux Lyon overlooking the historic district

Florentine, which overlooks the historic area. Several of Lyon's most prestigious hotels are here.

This area is long and only a few short blocks wide. It rests between the Saône River and the steep Fourvière hillside where the basilica and roman ruins are.

Positives of staying in Vieux Lyon: The most notable benefit is the charm of this area. There are no major roads running through here, so traffic noise is minimal.

You are never more than a few steps from restaurants offering a wide array of cuisines.

Transportation is convenient. The funiculars to the top of Fourvière hill start out from central Vieux Lyon and the subway stops here as well.

Some of the lodging sits on the hillside offering relaxing views of the historic district below you.

Negatives of staying in Vieux Lyon: This is a popular destination for tourists visiting Lyon. Many tour groups and their guides work their way through the streets. Restaurants can be busy, especially the more notable bouchons.

Distance to Place Bellecour and the Tourist Office is greater than if you were staying on the Presqu'île. Also, distance, and time involved, to reach any of the main train stations is longer.

Properties to consider in Vieux Lyon		
Hotel Name	Rating	Website
La Loge du Vieux Lyon	4	www.Loges.fr
Le Gourguillon	4	www.LeGourguillon.fr
MiHotel Vieux Lyon	3.5	www.MiHotel.fr Note – there is more than one MiHotel in Lyon.

Properties to consider in Vieux Lyon		
Hotel Name	Rating	Website
Villa Florentine	5	www.VillaFlorentine.com
Villa Maïa	5	www.Villa-Maia.com

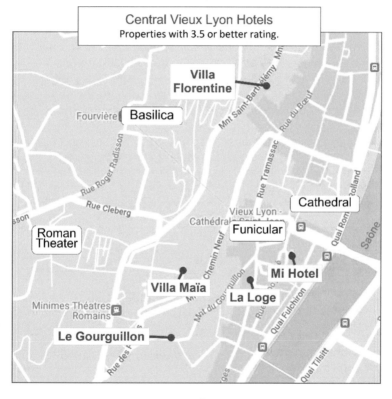

Central Vieux Lyon Hotels
Properties with 3.5 or better rating.

Place Carnot: Located south of Place Bellecour is Place Carnot, an attractive tree-lined square. This square is the home of a popular Christmas market in the winter, and, in the summer, a playground and outdoor sports are popular local attractions.

Place Carnot is adjacent to the busy train station, Gare de Lyon Perrache. This train station is generally used for transportation to nearby towns. This area is also close to another popular train station, Gare Jean-Mace.

Positives of staying near Place Carnot: The biggest plusses to staying in this area are convenience to transportation and affordability.

If you are planning on taking day trips by train, you are within easy reach of two stations which service local towns such as Vienne. The subway and tram systems both stop here.

The popular Confluence Museum and the point where the Saône and Rhône Rivers come together may easily be reached via the tram system from here.

Negatives of staying near Place Carnot: This section of Lyon is furthest from the historical area and the many attractions and museums found there. Noise can be a factor during the holiday season when the popular Christmas market is running. For a first-time visitor, this area should not be your first choice.

Properties to consider near Place Carnot		
Hotel Name	Rating	Website
Campanile Lyon Centre Gare Perrache	3.5	www.Campanile.com Then search for Lyon
Hôtel Alexandra Lyon	4	www.Hotel-Alexandra-Lyon.fr
Hôtel Des Remparts	3.5	www.HotelDesRempart-sLyon.com

Properties to consider near Place Carnot		
Hotel Name	Rating	Website
Hotel de Verdun 1882	4	www.HotelDeVerdun1882.com
Hôtel Mercure Lyon Centre Chateau Perrache	4	www.Mercure.Accor.com Note – this is a large chain with several properties with similar names.

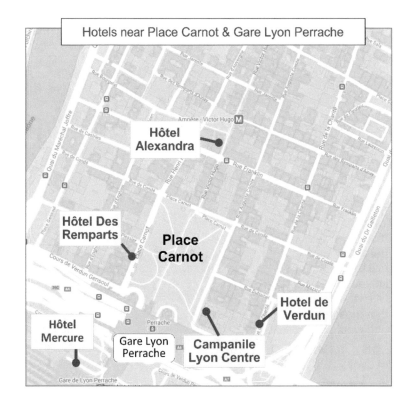

Hotels near Place Carnot & Gare Lyon Perrache

9: Nearby Day Trips from Lyon

Several opportunities for enjoyable and informative day trips out of town are available. These trips range from tasting some of the world's best wines to viewing ancient villages or Roman ruins.

This chapter outlines three general areas to consider. In addition to these, many other trip offerings are available and companies providing a broad range of tours are cited further in this chapter.

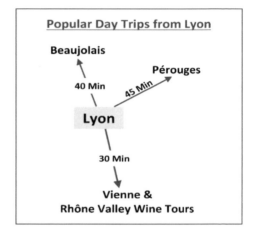

Popular Day Trips from Lyon

Beaujolais

Pérouges

40 Min

45 Min

Lyon

30 Min

Vienne &
Rhône Valley Wine Tours

Each of the destinations described here may be reached in under an hour. This limitation is in place with the assumption that most travelers don't want to devote most of the day in transit and would rather take time enjoying the tour and the destination.

Suggested day trips ranging between 4 hours to a full day out of Lyon:

- Vienne: Historic mid-size town with Roman roots.
- North Rhône Valley Wine: Visit family wineries along rolling hills which overlook the Rhône River. This can be combined with a trip to Vienne.

- Beaujolais: Hilly wine country just north of Lyon with many charming and historic villages.
- Pérouges: Ancient hilltop village with numerous shops and restaurants.

Vienne: Located a short distance south of Lyon is the charming and historic town of Vienne. This is a popular place to visit for many reasons; the ease of getting there, the Roman architecture, the setting alongside the Rhône River.

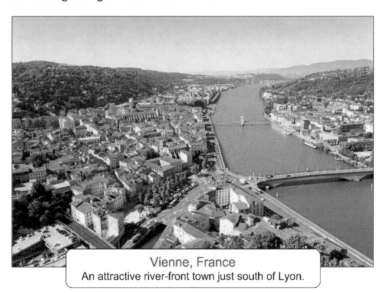

Vienne, France
An attractive river-front town just south of Lyon.

This town has a population of under 30,000 and has been occupied for thousands of years. Vienne boasts a medieval heritage which is evident along every twist and turn as you stroll through the narrow streets.

If your schedule allows, consider coming here on a Saturday morning. One of France's largest outdoor markets is set up here with nearly 3 kilometers of stands to browse. For many, this is a food lovers paradise.

Consider combining a visit to Vienne with a tour of local wineries. The North Rhône Valley wineries, Côte-Rôtie wines are some of the best in the world. To do this, it is helpful to join one of many group tours which depart out of Lyon.

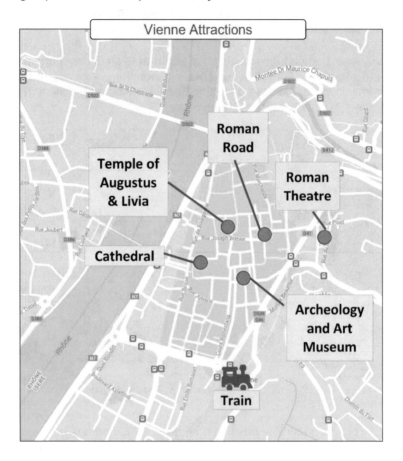

Vienne Attractions

Sites to visit in Vienne: Most of the key attractions in Vienne are in close proximity and can easily be reached on foot after only a short walk.

- Temple of Augustus and Livia. Built in 1st century BC, this monument sits in a square I the historic center of Vienne.

- Theater Antique. Large open-air Roman theater. Jazz concerts are held here every summer.

- Roman Road. Located in the city garden, you can view and walk a portion of the ancient Roman road. Look for the Archeological Gardens of Cybele.

- Saint-Maurice Cathédral. Beautiful and expansive cathedral and grounds built in the 11th century with Gothic design.

- Museum of Fine Art and Archeology. Expansive collection of art and antiquities from the Roman and Gallic periods.

- Roman Circus. View the tall stone monument which was once the center of many events in Vienne. (A bit of a walk – consider taking the city tram).

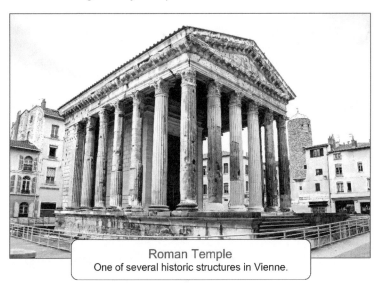

Roman Temple
One of several historic structures in Vienne.

Train to Vienne: This is an easy town to reach by train from Lyon. There is generally no need to join a tour if you like to set your own schedule. The train station in Vienne is close to the historic center and is an easy walk into town.

Trains depart Lyon approximately every 30 minutes. The ride can take 30 to 45 minutes, depending on which train you take. Take note of the station you depart Lyon from. Trains to Vienne from Lyon depart from 3 different stations: Part-Dieu, Jean Mace, and Lyon-Perrache,

Vienne City Tram. During the spring and summer seasons, an enjoyable city tram makes a circuit through the city. This can be beneficial as it takes you to the hillside overlooking Vienne and to the cathedral. Tickets may be purchased at the Vienne Tourist Office.

Rhône Valley Wine Tours: Stretching for 60 kilometers (37 miles) along the Rhône River Valley is the wine area referred to as North Rhône Valley. This area specializes in Syrah grapes which primarily produce rich red wines. Some of France's oldest vineyards may be found here. Vienne sits at the northern end of this wine region and there are over 1,800 wine growers. (Most do not have open wine tasting rooms).

North Rhône Valley Wines
Explore beautiful chateaux and fine wine on a Côte Rôtie /
North Rhône wine tour.

The wines grown closest to the town of Vienne are of the Côtie-Rôtie appellation[23]. These vineyards are striking in appearance as they are on steep hillsides rising from the river.

> Many full-day wine tours departing from Lyon also include a visit to Vienne.

Some, but not all, of the wineries here are open to the public. It is important, if you are traveling on your own, to check first before venturing off to these facilities. Many wineries are open only to tour groups, which provides a distinct advantage to joining one of these tours. These wineries range from small, family-owned, operations to large facilities with expansive chateaux.

If you prefer, many of the leading wines from here are represented in shops found in Vienne.

How to get here: Traveling to this area cannot be done by train unless you plan on sticking to visiting wineries with outlets within the town of Vienne. To visit the rolling hills with their many vineyards and wineries, you will need to rent a car or join one of the many available tours.

Several tour companies are listed later in this chapter and in the appendix of this guide.

Beaujolais Wine Country: A short distance north of Lyon is the Beaujolais wine region, an area of gentle rolling hills and numerous enchanting villages. This area is large and stretches north to the small city of Mâcon where the Burgundy wine region begins.

This Beaujolais region was first cultivated by the Romans and has been producing wine for over 2,000 years. The wines here

---

[23] Appellation Description: A wine's appellation, such as Côte-Rôtie, is the name of the specific geographical area where a wine is grown.

Route des Vins du Beaujolais

are typically made from Gamay grapes which is low in tannins, resulting in a slightly fruitier wine than those found along the Rhône valley. Most of the wines produced her are red and today there are twelve appellations.[24]

The Village of Oingt
A delightful spot in the heart of the Beaujolais wine region.

Visitors to this area will find over 1,000 growers and 60 villages. Most of the growers are small operations and do not have open tasting rooms. The village of Oingt is a great focal point for visiting here as the attractive hillside location offers not only great views but several tasting rooms as well. This village falls into the category of Beaux Villages, France's designation for the most beautiful villages.

---

[24] Beaujolais Details and Website: If wish to obtain an in depth understanding of Beaujolais wines, go to www.Beaujolais.com. This site provides excellent details on the appellations, and the "Route des Vins du Beaujolais."

A trip to the Beaujolais region will require a minimum of 4 hours and should be done either as a self-drive tour or joining one of the many tours out of Lyon. Visiting this area would, ideally, include stops at one or more of the family wineries [25] and at least one historic village. Many of the wineries are tucked away on back, winding roads and would be easy to miss without a knowledgeable guide and, another selling point for the tour companies is most of them have made arrangements with small family wineries for private tastings.

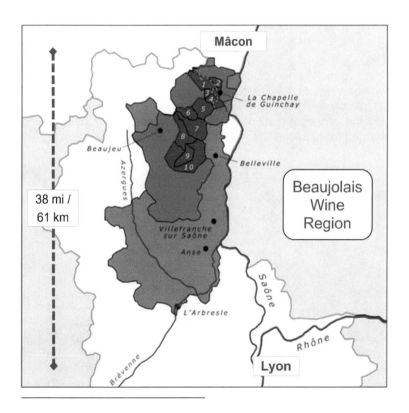

---

[25] Tour Visits to Wineries: Many of the tour operators will have arrangements to take groups into family owned and operated tasting rooms which are not otherwise open to the public.

How to get here: Travel considerations to this area are like traveling to the North Rhône Valley region. Trains do not service the villages, so you need to consider either renting a car or taking a tour.

Maps of the wineries may be found at the Lyon Tourist Office or specialty web sites such as www.CellarTours.com and general tour sites such as www.Viator.com or www.GetYourGuide.com.

Pérouges: A short distance northeast from Lyon is Pérouges, a walled town of 1,300 citizens which dates to nearly 2,500 BC. Originally a farming community, it played an important role in the silk industry during the 1800's as it is situated along the important trading route between Lyon and Geneva.

Pérouges
Ancient hilltop village just east of Lyon.

Today, Pérouges is labeled as one of France's Beaux Villages and it has become a popular spot for tourists. It is one of the most authentic medieval towns you can find. When you come here, you will see ancient cobblestone streets, city walls, medieval architecture, a fortified church, and numerous restaurants and shops.

Two cautions: This is a true village and not a typical tourist destination. The result is what you will find is mostly quiet cobblestone streets and a few small shops and restaurants. A visit won't take long, but you will have experienced a beautiful, but small, and extremely photo worthy locale. Also, the steep cobblestone lanes can be problematic to individuals with mobility issues.

How to get here: Traveling to Pérouges is easy to do and many tours out of Lyon are also available. Some of the tours to Pérouges include visits to Beaujolais wineries as an added plus.

Taking the train to Pérouges is easy and trains depart Lyon frequently each day.

- Trains to Pérouges depart from Lyon's Part-Dieu station.
- Travel time takes 30 to 45 minutes each way, depending on which train you board. Caution – some schedules require you to make a change of trains along the way. Look for trains which are direct.
- Purchase tickets to "Meximieux Pérouges" station.
- When arriving at Meximieux Pérouges, the station is a 20-minute uphill walk to the village. Often, you can find taxis to eliminate this hike.

Tour Companies for area Day Trips: Joining a tour to visit each of the locations described in this chapter can be beneficial. A list of several companies which provide small group and private tours follows. There is a substantial overlap in tour offerings across the providers so conducting some comparison shopping can be helpful.

Small group tours can be fun and, unless you have specific needs or limited budget, should be considered. These tours tend to be in a van with less than ten passengers. The tour guides will provide information which you might otherwise miss and take you to locations which you could not do on your own. Another plus is meeting other travelers who are often from different parts of the world. Finding tours in English is rarely a problem.

Most tour companies provide half-day and full-day tours. They also tend to provide tours to each of the locations recommended here.

Sample Area Tour Company Listings:

- En.VisiterLyon.com. This site is affiliated with the Lyon Tourist Office and offers a wide variety of tours out of Lyon. Many of these tours can be purchased at the Lyon Tourist Office or online in advance.

- Viator.com. This company is directly affiliated with TripAdvisor.com. This provides an advantage of being able to find numerous reviews about their tour offerings online. These tours need to be booked in advance online.

- UniqueToursFactoy.com. Offers small group, half-day tours. They strive to include unique elements into their tours such a cooking class when taking their Beaujolais Villages tour.

- ToursByLocals.com. Private full-day tours which can be customized to fit your needs. Pick up is directly at your Lyon hotel.

- Kanpai-Tourisme.com. Offers a wide variety of small group and private tours. Most of their tour offers are full-day and they often depart from Place Bellecour.

10: Day Trips Further Afield

If you are adventurous and do not mind devoting a large part of your day to transportation, several enjoyable train trips out of Lyon can be considered. Listed below are three options out of many.

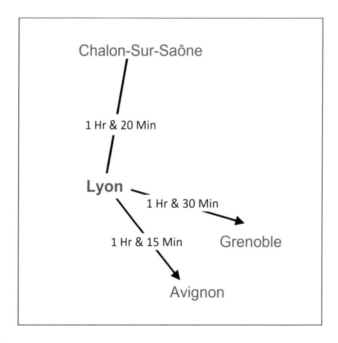

Three destinations are recommended which fit the important criteria of: (a) can be reached in under 90 minutes each way, (b) offer the visitor a wide range of sights, and (c) the train stations in the destination towns are convenient to main attractions.

Chalon-sur-Saône: As the town's name implies, this attractive small city of 45,000 is located on the Saône River. It is also in the heart of Burgundy wine country, a short distance north of Lyon and close to the popular village of Beaune.

Chalon-sur-Saône is best known as the birthplace of Photography. This history is recognized with a museum dedicated to early photography including two-million photographs and numerous artifacts.

The historical center and riverfront are enjoyable areas to explore on foot. The number of river boats which make this a stop attests to this. Don't come here for major historical sites as they are limited. Come here for a small-city experience with minimal tourism.

Chalon-sur-Saône
An attractive small city on the Saône River.

For most individuals, a few hours in town will cover the bases. More time will be needed if you wish to use this as a springboard to the wineries in this southern section of Burgundy. Several tasting rooms (Caves) may be found in town where local wines may be sampled and purchased.

Traveling to Chalon-sur-Saône from Lyon: Trains are recommended from Lyon or Beaune. Travel time is typically a little over one hour each way. Trains to Chalon from Lyon depart out of the Lyon Part Dieu station.

When arriving at the train station in Chalon-sur-Saône, it is a 15-to-20-minute walk to the oldest, more notable areas of town. Taxis are often available. Consider taking a taxi out to Cathédrale Saint-Vincent which is situated at the far end of the historical area.

City Website: www.Achalon.com

Avignon, France: This is an appealing medieval city on the Rhône River, in the heart of the Provence region. Come here to tour beautiful lavender fields or explore the city's numerous sights. Also, consider staying here for a night or two. At risk of being cliché' this place is awesome.

Avignon, France
Popular medieval city on the Rhône River.

Crowd Caution

Avignon is very popular and during the summer months can be crowded.

There is little doubt as to why so many river cruises make this one of their banner stops. Avignon is a spread-out midsize city with a city population of over 90,000 and the overall metro area has a population of over 400,000.

While this is sizeable, the historic center of Avignon holds most of the visual delights which first-time visitors come to see. The huge exception to this is the nearby lavender fields which require a drive out to them or a tour.

When visiting here, plan on spending a full day. If you travel in from Lyon by train, starting early out from Lyon is advisable. Once you are in town, most of the popular sights are near one another.

Avignon's history, like so much else in the region, dates back to the Roman era. In the 14th century it was the seat of Catholic Popes, the papacy. The Palais des Papes, which was primary building complex for the papacy, is an imposing fortress and should be at the top of your list to visit.

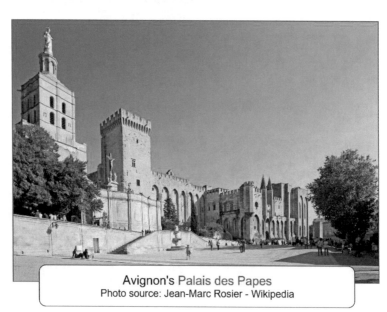

Avignon's Palais des Papes
Photo source: Jean-Marc Rosier - Wikipedia

Helpful Resources: To help ensure you have an enjoyable visit to Avignon, consider using one or both of the following:

- Websites: Avignon's tourist office provides substantial guidance including information on tours, shopping and restaurants: www.Avignon-Tourisme.com. Another good website to explore is www.Avignon-Et-Provence.com.

- App: The best Android and Apple app currently available on Avignon is the Avignon Maps and Walks by GPS my City. There is a modest charge to unlock all of the features.

Points of Interest: A few highlights of Avignon include:
- Palais des Papes – huge fortress and cathedral. Former residence of Catholic Pontiffs during the 14th century. This is the largest Gothic palace in the world.
- Basilique Saint Pierre: A 14th century Gothic church in the heart of town.
- The Saint Bénézet Bridge. Also known as "the Bridge of Avignon" and listed as a Unesco World Heritage Site. Walk out on this 14th century bridge which takes you over the Rhône River.
- Pkace de l'Horlage: A large plaza in the heart of Avignon's historic center. In addition to the 19th century City Hall and a former Cardinal's palace. A great spot for dining and shopping.
- Rocher des Doms: A park which overlooks the city and river below.
- Avignon City Walls: These ramparts are the world's second longest city walls. Several access points may be found in the city.

Travel to Avignon from Lyon: If you are driving, it is slightly over two hours each way. Although this drive is a bit lengthy, it is along a prominent highway which follows the Rhone.

   Train travel is generally the best way to reach Avignon but take care as this can be tricky given that Avignon has two stations. There is a central Gare d'Avignon Centre station close to town, but only slower trains head here and a train journey from Lyon can take over two hours each way. The quickest train trip, with is just a little over an hour, is to travel to the Avignon TGV station. (TGV is France's highspeed train network) This TGV station is on the edge of town and is not within walking distance of central Avignon. From this station, you will want to catch ground transportation such as a taxi, to reach the heart of town.

Grenoble, France: When traveling, you occasionally come upon a town or area which prompts you to think, "I could live here." For the author, this was the feeling he and his wife had on their first visit. It is a relaxing and beautiful small city which just calls out to the visitor to stay a while.

The Le Bastille Cable Car and Grenoble

Grenoble is at the foothills of the Alps and is the charming city of Grenoble. Despite being a bit off of the beaten path, this is a sizeable city. The city proper has a population of roughly 160,000 and the metro area's population is over 700,000. This city deserves a separate guide as it has a bit of everything including museums, outdoor activities, even a tram system.

Grenoble calls itself "The Capital of the Alps." And, as some validation to this, Grenoble held the Winter Olympics in 1968. The easy access to the city by trains and the airport (The airport has since faded somewhat), along with the proximity to many mountain ski areas, made this something of a natural locale. Oddly, elevation is only 1,640 feet (400 meters), so the city itself does not feel at all alpine.

Grenoble has an extensive tram system.
Photo source: Gwenn Boussard - Wikimedia Commons

Today, this is a growing metro area and has developed a reputation as a center for research and innovation. With the many large labs in the area, nearly 20% of the area's residents work in technology.

As a visitor coming for a day trip, you have the option of exploring the town centre or even taking a gondola up to a medieval fortress. In town there is a large fine arts museum and large city park. If you enjoy outdoor activities, you have choices ranging from casual hikes to alpine skiing. However, if you are coming in just for a day trip, it is difficult to fit in substantial time to do this.

For many casual visitors, the Old Town is an excellent place to start. You will find quaint pedestrian shopping streets lined with shops and restaurants.

Detailed Website: Grenoble's Tourist Office provides an excellent website which outlines how to get around in town and where each attraction is. www.Grenoble-Tourisme.com.

Traveling to Grenoble from Lyon: Most trains take about one hour and twenty minutes and there are frequent departures every day. Almost all trains depart from Lyon's Part Dieu station. When you arrive in Grenoble, the Gare de Grenoble can be anywhere from a fifteen to thirty-minute walk to the most popular sites. The trams do stop in front of the train station and, once you purchase a day pass from the ticket kiosk, it is easy to travel around town. Grenoble's website www.Grenoble-Tourisme.com provides excellent details on ticket cost and how to purchase tickets and passes.

Appendix: Helpful Online References

To help you expand your knowledge of this area, several online reference sites are listed here. Lyon and the neighboring towns of Vienne, Pérouges, and others are popular places to visit so there is a wealth of material which can help in planning your trip.

Following is a list of online references about this city and area. The purpose of this list is to enhance your understanding of this area before embarking on your trip. Any online search will result in the websites outlined here plus many others. These are listed as they are professionally done and do not only try to sell you tours.

I.	Lyon City and Area Websites.
Website Name	Website address and description
Bouchons	The following sites provide helpful information on Lyon's bouchons, the cuisine offered, and where to find the best ones. - www.MyFrenchGuide.com – go into the page specific to bouchons. - OnlyLyon.com – go into the Lyon restaurants section.
Lyon City Card	www.LyonCityCard.com Details on the city card and provisions to purchase the cards online in advance of your trip.
Maison Canuts	www.MaisonDesCanuts.fr Learn about Lyon's silk trade and explore available workshops and tours specific to the silk industry.

I.	Lyon City and Area Websites.
Website Name	**Website address and description**
Only Lyon	www.OnlyLyon.com or www.VisiterLyon.com Helpful information to visitors on what to see, events, and tours.
This Is Lyon	www.ThisIsLyon.Fr City-sponsored website providing substantial information on the city, tours, events, museums, historical sites, and more.
U.S News	Travel.USNews.com/Lyon_France Detailed information on Lyon's weather, when to visit and what to see when visiting Lyon.
You Tube	Several helpful videos available. One of the best is under the search term "Places to see in Lyon."
Wikipedia	www.Wikipedia.org OR simply do a search for Lyon and this site will appear on most search results pages. Detailed information on Lyon's history and the city's early development.

II.	Lyon Museums and Major Attractions
Museum / Attraction	**Website**
Beaux-Arts Museum	www.MBA-Lyon.fr
Cinema Miniatures	www.MuseeMiniatureetCinema.fr
Confluence Museum	www.MuseeDesConfluence.fr

II. Lyon Museums and Major Attractions	
Museum / Attraction	Website
Contemporary Arts	www.Mac-Lyon.com
Fourvière Hill and Basilica	www.Fourviere.org.en
Gadagne History and Puppetry Museums	Gadagne.Musees.Lyon.fr
Lumière Institute	www.Institut-Lumiere.org
Murals and Frescos	En.Lyon-France.com/Discover-Lyon Helpful information on the large outdoor murals found around Lyon. Murals are one of many attractions detailed in this site.
Textiles and Decorative Arts Museum	www.MuseeDesTissus.fr
Traboules	www.LyonTraboules.net or ThisIsLyon.fr/Things-to-do Each of these sites provide information and maps on Lyon's traboules.

III. Area Villages and Towns	
Area	Website address and Description
Oingt	En.Wikipedia.org/wiki/Oingt Background information on the history of this medieval village in the Beaujolais area.
Pérouges	www.MyItchyFeet.com/Visit-Perouges A well-written blog on Pérouges with photos, detailing traveling to this historic site and what to look for when visiting.

III.	Area Villages and Towns
Area	Website address and Description
Vienne	www.France-Voyage.com Then search for "Vienne" Detailed information on Vienne, how to get there, tours, restaurants, and what to do when visiting this historic town.
Best Day Trips	www.TrainLine.com Search for Lyon once you enter the site. There is a helpful list of recommended day trips from Lyon.

IV.	Transportation Information and Tickets
Website Name	Website Address & Description
Airport Train	Store.LyonAeroPorts.com Purchase tickets for the Lyon airport "Rhône Express" train and view current schedules.
French Train / SNCF	www.SNCF.com/en
Lyon Metro	www.MetroEasy.com/Lyon-Metro.html Detailed info on Lyon's subway and tram system including maps.
Train Ticket Resellers	Several services enable you to purchase train tickets online prior to your trip, including: - RailEurope.com - Rome2rio.com - TrainLine.com - Eurorailways.com
Welcome Pickups	www.WelcomePickups.com Book private transportation from the Lyon airport to your hotel.

V.	Tour and Hotel Booking Sites
Company	Website address and Description
Hotel Sites	Numerous online sites enable you to review and book hotels online. Most of these sites also resell tours. - Booking.com - Hotels.com - Expedia.com - Travelocity.com
Only Lyon	EnVisiterLyon.com This site, associated with the city of Lyon, provides numerous tours to and outside Lyon.
Tour Resellers	Many companies, such as the ones listed here, provide a full variety of tours to Lyon as well as day tours. - GetYourGuide.com - ToursByLocals.com - Viator.com - WorldTravelGuide.net
Trip Advisor	www.TripAdvisor.com One of the most comprehensive sites on hotels and tours. Direct connection with Viator, a tour reseller.

Index

Airport Tram 31
Apps to Download 8
Arrondissements 13
Astronomical Clock...............43
Avignon, France 117
Basilica Notre-Dame 35
Beaujolais Tours 109
Beaux Arts Museum 50
Bellecour Plaza 48
Bicycle Rentals.....................87
Bouchons 70
Cathédrale............................43
Chalon-sur-Saône 116
Cinema Minatures 41
City Passes 88
Climate in Lyon 21
Confluence Museum 56
Contemporary Arts 64
Croix-Rousse Tunnel...........55
Fine Arts Museum 50
Fourviere Hill 35
Fun Facts about Lyon...........20
Funiculars............................80
Gadagne Musées................45
History Museum 45
Hop-On Bus 82
Hotel de Ville 17, 52
Jewish Deportation Museum 59
Lugdunum Museum..............39
Lumière Museum..................61
Lyon Airport.........................29
Lyon City Card 88
Murals 77
Musee Lumiere 61

Museum Card......................91
Oingt, France 110
One-Day Itinerary................23
Palais des Papes 118
Parc de la Tete d'Or 63
Pérouges Day Trip 112
Place Bellecour 48
Place Carnot 47
Place des Terreaux 52
Points of Interest List...........32
Presqu'île Overview 17
Presquile Points of Interest ..46
Puppetry Museum 45
Resistance Museum.............59
Rhone Express....................31
Rhone Valley Tours...........108
Roman Ampitheater 54
Roman Theater 40
Roman Theater Museum......39
Silk Saint-Georges 74
Silk Shops 73
Sports Stadium....................21
Subways & Trams 83
The Little Prince 20
Three Gauls Roman Theater54
Tourist Office........................ 7
Tours of Lyon 92
Traboules. 66
Train Stations 26
Tunnel Croix-Rousse...........55
Vienne Day Trip 105
Vieux Lyon 18
Walking Distances...............78
WWII Resistance Museum ...59
Zoo......................................63

Starting-Point Travel Guides

www.StartingPointGuides.com

This guidebook on Lyon is one of several current and planned *Starting-Point Guides*. Each book in the series is developed with the concept of using one enjoyable city as your basecamp and then exploring from there.

Current guidebooks are for:

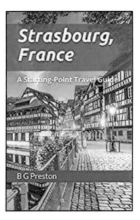

- Bordeaux, France, Plus the surrounding Gironde River region
- Cologne & Bonn Germany
- Dijon, France Plus the Burgundy Region
- Geneva, Switzerland Including the Lake Geneva area.
- Gothenburg, Sweden Plus the Västra Götaland region.
- Lille, France and the Nord-Pas-de-Calais Area.
- Lucerne, Switzerland, Including the Lake Lucerne area.
- Nantes, France and the western Loire Valley.
- Reims and Épernay, France the heart of the Champagne Region.
- Salzburg, Austria and the Salzburg area.
- Strasbourg, France, and the central Alsace region.
- Stuttgart, Germany and the and the Baden-Württemberg area.
- Toledo, Spain: The City of Three Cultures
- Toulouse, France, and the Haute-Garonne area.

Updates on these and other titles may be found on the author's Facebook page at: www.Facebook.com/BGPreston.author

Feel free to use this Facebook page to provide feedback and suggestions to the author or email to: cincy3@gmail.com

Made in United States
Troutdale, OR
12/06/2023